From The Cotton Fields to the Capitol

My destiny with diabetes

FLORENE LINNEN

Mamaroneck, N.Y. 10543

Copyright © 2017 by Florene Linnen

ALL RIGHTS RESERVED

No part of this book may be transmitted or reproduced in any form electronic, mechanical, photocopying, recording or otherwise without written permission from the copyright owner.

Library of Congress Control Number: 2017909822

ISBN: 978-0-692-90972-0

Edited by Dorothy L. Carr

Published by TOOO Expressions
P.O. Box 144
Mamaroneck, N.Y. 10543

DEDICATION

To my mother and father, Pauline and Silas Jackson, you instilled in me a strong foundation, nuggets of wisdom, and love for all people. I appreciate you even more today. You would've been pleased.

To my sisters Rose Hurell, Ruth Priest, Gertrude Thompson, Calethia Franklin, Louverta Ruise, Mary Ruise and Phyllys McKnight; to my brothers Jessie Washington, Thomas Jackson, Frank Madison Jackson; thanks for your support.

To Margaret Carr who was my running buddy from the beginning. She was a faithful supporter to the very end. Rest in peace.

To my husband, Herbert Lee Linnen, who for 55 years, has supported all of my efforts. I thank God for you.

CONTENTS

ACKNOWLEDGMENTS VII
ABOUT THIS BOOK IX

PART I

WHO IS FLORENE LINNEN?

1 - A Strong Foundation 3
2 - Building A Family 24
3 - Answering the Call 37
4 - A Willing Worker 43
5 - Community 49
6 - Taking a Stand 55
7 - Miracles in My Life 59
8 - Who Is Florene Linnen? 73

PART II

THE GEORGETOWN COUNTY DIABETES C.O.R.E GROUP

9 - Defining the Diabetes CORE Group 103
10 - Diabetes CORE Group Activities 123
11 - Awards & Recognition 146
12 - 10 - Year Milestone 157

PART III

SUMMARY

At A Glance 163

ACKNOWLEDGMENTS

It gives me great pleasure in expressing my deepest gratitude to the many people who believed in my work and joined forces with me to create change for people in need and the people who embraced my goal to share my experience with the world in the hopes of encouraging other people to do the same.

My gratitude goes to my children (Michael, Andy, Mark, Michelle, Tranja, Herbie and Josh). Thank you for all your support and encouragement.

Thanks to my Aunt Maggie who was always full of encouragement with every project and event I held. She would always call her children to let them know and she would call me and let me know of any feedback she had heard afterwards.

I am grateful for the support of uncle Bubba
Thanks to Tressia Devlin. I am forever grateful to you for inviting me to that life changing *Diabetes Today* workshop, in Myrtle Beach, that started it all.

I am thankful to the rural communities of Georgetown County, South Carolina for supporting me and participating in my projects educating people about diabetes. I do not have adequate words to express my gratitude. So I will just say thanks.

Thank you to the current and former Board of Directors of the Georgetown County Diabetes CORE Group for sticking with me and helping me to develop my leadership skills.

My gratitude goes to my daughter-in-law, Joyce Linnen. I am so appreciative of your technical skills and how you generously donate them to our cause.

Many thanks to Pat Haynes and C.J. Cohen for helping me to review the material for this book. You are true gems.

I am grateful to my niece, Lucinda, who pushed me and motivated me, until I began to write. She believed in me. Lucinda helped me to compile and organize this information which I wanted to share and put it in the form of a book. Thanks for helping me to get it all together.

ABOUT THIS BOOK

From a small acorn comes a huge oak tree with lots of branches going in different directions when it is planted in an environment that nurtures it and provides what it needs to grow. It is a very modest beginning.

In the same manner, a small idea, when properly nurtured in a suitable environment, can produce amazing results.

Like an acorn, someone planted a small idea, in my mind, in the form of an invitation to attend a workshop. The environment of my mind was nourished with passion, enthusiasm and love for people. What resulted was not just the intended improvement of health in my community, but inspiration for other communities and recognition in various forms from all over.

People continually invite me to events to speak and share about my organization. They are always so amazed at our results. It was this interest that others have in the Georgetown County Diabetes CORE Group that inspired me to write this book. I wanted to share the information beyond where I could go in person.

I spoke about this book for years. I kept saying that I wanted to write a book. I wanted to tell people what I did so that they would do the same or similar. I wanted them to know that it was possible for anyone.

The book turned out to be a bigger job than we imagined. But just like my work with diabetes, people joined in and helped me. And I was amazed at the interest. I was asked continually, "When is the book coming?"

When my niece asked me in January of 2014, how far along I was, I told her that I had not started, yet. She said, "What? I thought you were half done by now!" So she said, "I am going to help you get started."

She asked me why I wanted to write this book. I explained why – because I want other people to know that it can be done and give them some ideas.

So with that, we made an appointment to start work on my book. I didn't know where to begin, but together, we got started. And now, I want to share with you the story of what went into the creation of the Georgetown County Diabetes CORE Group in Georgetown, South Carolina, and how anyone can do it.

Now, read on because I am going to tell you a story that had its beginning over 70 years ago.

PART I

WHO IS

FLORENE LINNEN?

1

A Strong Foundation

I am going to tell you a story. The story is an autobiography, but not what you would expect. I am not a writer, but I am a story teller. I love to talk. So I am going to tell you a story which began decades ago. This story answers a question that I get a lot - "How did you do it?" Do what? Create the Georgetown County Diabetes CORE Group. Here is my answer.

Humble Beginnings

In the still of the night, down a dark dirt road, stood a four room house out in the rural section of Georgetown County known as Oatland. The folks that lived in that house were descendants of former slaves.

Those slaves performed many back breaking tasks and endured severe punishment because of those who dared to rebel against unfair treatment. They had to work out in the fields whether they were sick or well. Their work days started before sunrise and ended after sunset each day.

There was a handsome young man and a beautiful young lady who met by chance and started a courtship. They were descended from those hard working slaves. Eventually, they fell deeply in love. After dating for a while, they decided to get married. They knew that it was a chance they had to take because they really wanted to be together as man and wife. So, they tied the knot.

This couple lived in that four-room house I mentioned above. They were very grateful because while they were poor, this was *their* house and *they* were free. They were my future parents, Pauline Myers Jackson and Silas Jackson.

Not long after getting married, they started raising a family. Along the way, they experienced many days of hardship including not being able to put food on the table to feed their children.

Pauline and Silas took solace, however, in knowing that with their strong faith in God, they would be able to take on life's challenges and the stumbling blocks they would encounter. They always remembered the teachings that were passed on to them from their parents: "Always keep God First." And they kept God first in everything they did. They were confident that God would provide for them and see them through their hard times.

They passed this belief on to their children. As time went on, Pauline gave birth to their third child. Who would ever have guessed what destiny had in store for this baby girl? She was a bundle of joy to the family, when she arrived.

The third child of Pauline and Silas Jackson was born on January 3, 1943, in the Oatland community of Georgetown, S.C. Altogether, ten children were born to Pauline and Silas - 7 girls and 3 boys.

This third child came on the scene early on a Sunday morning, and weighed only 3lbs. The temperature outside was 52 degrees and the sky was clear with no chance of rain. It was very cold on the outside. But the small house, in which they lived, was also cold on the inside. You see, it had no insulation to keep the drafts out. The pot belly, trash burning heater, with the tin stove pipes exiting through an opening on the wall of the house, expelled the smoke up into the blue sky.

For a moment, the couple had forgotten all about the many struggles they had been through up to this point in their lives. But the struggles were very real for them. Never the less, they believed that this child as well as their other children came into this world for a reason.

As this child grew, they noticed that she possessed some unique qualities about her that were different from the other children. She stood out among all the other children in the household. Shyness was, definitely, not one of her attributes. And she was always eager to speak her mind, especially if she thought something was unfair. She was very strong minded, independent and always full of confidence.

You never found her backing down from others. If she believed in what she was saying, it was hard to convince her otherwise. As she grew older, she could multitask because she was very organized. Most of all, she was very sociable and had compassion for others.

There was definitely a reason she was born. In fact there are many. The reasons can be found in books and magazines and newspapers around the country. They can be found in the diabetes statistics in Georgetown, S.C and other cities that have benefited from her unique qualities that made her stand out from the other children.

This child was named Florene Jackson; she was later nicknamed Flo. Yes, that's how it all started for me, Florene (Jackson) Linnen.

I love people. And I am committed to helping as many people as I can to live better and live longer.

The Environment

For my parents, growing up had been a struggle. Their parents had had to make do with whatever little they had, as well, in order to raise them and their siblings. Now, my parents found themselves having the same experiences. It was, now, their turn to walk in their parents' shoes.

As was the case for most of the neighborhood, I grew up poor. We lived in a house that had no running water. Our family had a pump from which to get water to drink, cook and wash clothes, etc. The pump had a handle for pumping and it was set up outside.

Once or twice a year the packing on the pump would wear out and needed to be replaced. As I recall, many times we would be without a pump for days because my father had to walk into town to buy a new packing. The town was several miles away. That would leave me and my siblings taking turns carrying water from a nearby neighbor's house several times a day.

Since there was no running water, there was also no bathroom within the little four room house in which we lived.

During those days, all families used an outhouse as a toilet. Our outhouse was built by my father. The outhouse had to be cleaned once a week with bleach and soapy water. Even the floor had to be scrubbed. It was taking what you had and making the best of it. My sisters and I took turns completing the chores around the house, including the cleaning of the outhouse.

Laundry was a team effort. When wash day came around, the big black pot (outside) was filled with water. Then it was surrounded by fire wood and the wood was lit. I remember us taking turns carrying buckets of water to fill the wash pot to wash the dirty laundry. If the laundry was very dirty, they were placed inside the big, black pot, along with the soap, to boil the dirt out of them. There was no washing machine with its hot water setting.

On the back porch was the tin metal wash tub along with a wash board. They were used to scrub the clothes that were not quite as dirty as the ones that had to be placed in the boiling water in the big black pot surrounded by burning firewood. Firewood was placed under the pot all day to boil the clothes to get them clean.

Once a year, after we had worked very hard all year long, we celebrated with a tradition. Two hogs were killed and butchered. The meat was shared with the other families in our small community to be prepared for their families. That was a joyous occasion for everyone.

Who's the Boss?

Silas had a son before he met Pauline, so I actually had 4 brothers. My oldest brother lived with his grandparents, on his mother's side, but we all played and did things together as a family.

With 10 children in our house to raise, my parents had their hands full. When my mother or father spoke, there was no backtalk. And my father could just look at me and I knew I had better behave myself. My father would let us know that while he would play with us, he was still the boss. It was pretty easy for my parents to raise us, even though there were so many of us. Why? Because we respected our parents and we were obedient children.

We had a very strong childhood. My parents were very strict. They believed in children listening, learning the structure of a good family life, learning manners and having respect for their elders as well as respect for people, in general.

Not only that, my parents taught us to have common sense. And believe me, sense is not always common. I can still hear them say:

- "If you have one dress, wash it, iron it, and hang it up until time to wear it again;"
- "The important thing is *get an education*;"
- "Don't be a dressed up dummy."

These were some of the nuggets of wisdom taught to us by Pauline and Silas Jackson.

They were poor. However, what my parents lacked in money, they made up for in wisdom. My father taught us love, honesty, respect and to be hard workers. It was important to them that they taught us how to treat people and also that manners will take you anywhere; that we should owe no man anything. And they knew how to balance correction with compliments. "You all are the most beautiful girls there is." That is what they would say to us all of the time.

Old sayings are some of the things they instilled in me. And *my*, how those old sayings have impacted my life! I still, at age 74, try to be a good neighbor, respect people and I am willing to help others. I can remember my father saying, "Don't ever look down on people unless you are picking them up," - a worthy statement to remember, if there ever was one.

We didn't have much when I was growing up. Our entertainment was our father playing the guitar as we danced. My father loved to play the guitar. I remember, so well, a favorite song he loved to play called, *"Show Shoe Baby."* He played and we danced. We had so much fun dancing to the music my father played! It's a good thing we did because we didn't have any electricity, much less a TV. So, our options for entertainment were very limited.

Childhood was a happy time for me. My sisters and brothers and I played very well together. Because we didn't have a lot of money to spend on toys and gadgets, we used our minds and ingenuity to create fun. A lack of money led to an abundance of creativity and we got to be very creative.

Many hours of fun were provided by our handmade toys. We could have as many toys as we wanted. Our only limit was our imagination. The doll babies were made from grass pulled up out of the fields. After we pulled the grass up, it was then turned upside down, and dressed up. The roots of the grass were combed to make the doll baby's hair which we adorned with ribbons.

Now, that was great for the girls, but what about the boys? Well, no one was left out. We were a team. For the boys, we used an old can and a piece of board and made an old board wagon for my brothers to play with.

Yes, we were happy children. Like other kids in the area, we enjoyed clean innocent fun. In addition to making toys, we also enjoyed jumping rope, playing hop scotch, climbing trees, and playing marbles. Oh yes, we also played *school*. In fact, playing school was one of our favorite games. And every time we did, I was the teacher.

At one point, my father went into the Navy. So, we stayed with our grandparents - my father's parents - for a few years. Sometimes, we would get the shoe thrown at us by my granddaddy. You see, because my granddaddy worked nights, he needed to sleep during the day, which was when the children were wide awake. But with the children talking and playing, the noise would, often, wake him up. Being the teacher, and of course, in charge, definitely did not keep me from getting the shoe thrown at me. My granddaddy wasn't really trying to hit us. It was more of a warning - a way to get our attention. If he really wanted to hit us, he never would have missed.

Playing aside, there was one thing that we had to do. There was no discussion about it; no explaining, when it came time to go to church. We were required to go to church.

Every Sunday morning we had to attend Sunday school and stay at the church until church service was over. If we didn't go to church, then we were not allowed to visit our friends and play with them later that day. That was critical for us kids because Sunday was the only day of the week that children were allowed to play. The other days of the week were consumed by all of the chores that had to be done around the house. You have probably heard it said, "Train up a child in the way they should go…"

I am happy to say that my parents never went to a jail house or a court room for any of their children. And those old sayings, along with my parents' training, helped to lay the foundation for the work that I would do with the Georgetown County Diabetes CORE Group.

Those Cotton Pickin' Days

Needing to support his family, my father, of course, sought out work. He knew that finding a job would be hard, in the small rural community of Oatland, because everyone was struggling to take care of their families. He, also, wanted to be at home with his family. But in order to provide for his family, he had to go out and leave his family at home. So, he took the time and learned the mastery of farming from the older farmers in the community. This allowed him to be near his family while working to support them.

Our entire family pitched in. My father taught me how to hitch a mule to the plow and how to plow the rows. He also taught me how to saw wood and hitch up the wagon to carry the plow to the fields. I didn't mind it at all.

Life was a struggle for my parents, being young and starting their new family together. Although my father farmed for a living and planted food, that was no guarantee that we would have enough food to eat. Some seasons the fields didn't yield enough crops. This resulted in the food being rationed with the hope that it would last until the next growing season.

At a very young age (before my teen-age years), Pauline and Silas' 2 oldest children and I started working. We went to work for very low wages doing work such as picking beans, for 20 cents a basket. Even when it was cold and raining we still worked. We worked so that we could have money to buy clothes for school, but we also gave some of the money to the family, you know, for necessities.

One day when I was about 11 years old (give or take a year) my father came home and said that we - the children - were going to farm with a man for half of the money that the crop would bring in. Well, my mother didn't like it, but dad had spoken. That arrangement didn't last very long, however. By the time we harvested the crops, most of the money we would have gotten as our pay was already spent for life's necessities like kerosene to stay warm and food to eat. That was the end of that.

Since my early teens, I always tried to earn money, myself. I wanted to help my family. A 12 or 13-year old girl, in those days, had a few options. She could iron, mop and clean house to make a few dollars.

I remember that there was a man (Let's call him Mr. Jones.) who needed someone to do house work and take care of his baby. My mother asked which one of us would like to go. Well, I volunteered to go and babysit and do house work. My wages were $2.00/day.

It worked out well for a few weeks. And then, the child said something that would be a deal breaker. She said something like, "My daddy said you work like a nigger." Immediately, I said, "What?"

Little children innocently repeat what they hear grown-ups say. This little girl did not realize what she was saying and she repeated it, again. So, I responded, "This nigger is going home." And I headed for the door. As I was leaving, I told the older person in the house, "Bye." This incident was totally unexpected by the Jones'. After all, I was a very good worker. So, of course, she wanted to know what happened. I just said, "I'm going home." And with that, I left.

Well, as one might have expected, this caused a bit of an upset for the Jones family. Mr. Jones came to our house that very afternoon to try to fix things. My dad called me into the house. He asked me, "Do you want to go back?" I replied with a definite, "No." My father then said to Mr. Jones, "She doesn't want to go because my children are tough and they don't have to take that kind of talk from anybody because you, too, can be a *nigga*. That is someone *without* common sense. That's a *nigga*."

My father was a poor, but intelligent man. He knew that there was more to life than money. He raised us with that kind of mindset.

Subsequently, I still worked in homes, sometimes, for $2.00 a day - $10 a week. My children say, "No way I will work for $10.00 a week." In those days, however, you could buy a lot for ten dollars. Shoes, for instance, were very cheap. You could buy them for 1 dollar a pair.

In addition to working in homes, another way I earned money was "working in green tobacco." We stripped the ripe tobacco leaves from the tobacco stalk and tied them up, using *tobacco string*, to a special kind of stick made specifically for this purpose and appropriately named a *tobacco stick*. The stick of strung up tobacco would be put into a tobacco barn for curing. The cured tobacco would be sold at the market and used for cigarettes and other tobacco products.

Sometimes, we would "camp out." When we "camped out," we left home and stayed about a week at a time, in another town/city, on the farm where we were going to be working. Once, I was "camping out" in tobacco with my mother and one of my sisters. We worked for $7.00 a day. My sister and I would "hand tobacco" and my mother would "string" the tobacco onto a *tobacco stick*. Sometimes we "camped out" in Loris, S.C.

Other times we would "camp out" in Conway, S.C. Camping out was a common practice in the area where we lived.

Once, my parents let us go to work "camping out" in Loris, S.C. with a cousin. This cousin was a male and the adult in the group. Well, I was always one to stand up and speak out.

One night, we came in late. Now, we had to cook on an open fire in a fire place. So we had to take turns in using the fire and cooking our food. Usually, some of us would cook our food together to save time. My sister and I cooked our food together.

That night, it was our turn to cook first. My cousin, however, tried to pull rank on us being that he was older. He wanted to use the fire place first. Now, my older sister was always quiet. When anyone got into an argument with her, I would step in and handle the situation for her. Such was the case that night. An argument broke out between me and my adult cousin. My cousin exclaimed, "That gal isn't got any manners."

I knew that when I got home, my father was going to ask what happened. But he was a fair man. He would always give us a chance to tell our side of the story. And when he did, he would say, "Just keep in mind that you will get your switch, and don't get the smallest one in the woods. Because if you do, you will go back and get another one, until I feel like you got the right size." So, my father taught us to respect our elders; when older people speak, you must listen. I did, however, escape the beating that time because I was defending myself and my sister and we were in the right. I didn't have to get a switch that time.

Picking cotton is another way we earned money when I was young. It seemed like cotton fields were everywhere in South Carolina. We picked cotton for 3 cents a pound. That means we earned a mere $3.00 for every hundred pounds of cotton we picked. I could never pick 100 pounds of cotton. If memory serves me right, the highest I ever picked was 87 pounds.

It's funny because whoever we worked for that day would stop by the store with us earlier in the day and he would pay for whatever we got to eat. At the end of the day, when it was time to pay us, he would take back the money he spent on us earlier, before paying us that evening. If anything was left, you took it home and gave it to your parents. As you might guess, not much was left.

Working in pulp wood was big in our area. Many of the men, including my father, worked in pulp wood. They harvested the trees that were growing in the woods. Sometimes they were in the woods all day, but made no money because of the rainy weather. At times, the trucks would even get bogged down in the mud. But through it all, we remained a happy family. Our mind set was that we can do all things through Christ who strengthens us.

I remember one Easter when my father didn't work a lot, prior to Easter, due to the weather. So, my brother (Pauline and Silas' oldest son) went to Georgetown (the city) to buy an Easter outfit for me and my oldest sister. He and my father worked with pulp wood. My brother used money that he himself had earned to make the purchases. My brother, who was 16 years old, wanted to help and did the best he could. He bought me a black and white wedge heel shoe and a beige suit.

After Easter, however, my brother started calling the shoes, "Big Foot." My brother was always a teaser. He would tease you over the littlest things. His teasing was nothing major. After all, my parents taught us, as children, that we are "one." They wanted us to live together peacefully then and after they were gone and we did.

Always trying to do his best, one day, my father and his brothers came together and got the bright idea to plant tobacco for themselves. We children did not like it, but we knew better than to say anything.

After we started farming for ourselves, my father would pay us a small amount of money because we helped.

When it was time to harvest the crops, my brother who had bought me the Easter clothes, hated it - picking cotton and cropping tobacco. When the cotton or tobacco was sold, he would remind us, "I still don't like farming." My brother has since gone on to live with the Lord.

Early Education

When I think about those old sayings that my parents taught us, sometimes, other things come to mind. Those memories remind me of going to school in an old, one-room, wooden building with outdoor toilets. I am grateful that my children had better conditions when they were coming up and going to school.

In the old days, we walked to school. We also, had to gather wood in the winter months to maintain a fire in order to stay warm. And yes, some days we fought, as children sometimes do.

I remember one time when I thought I was going to be beaten up by a kid at school. We went outside to gather wood for the wood-burning stove that we used to heat the room as well as heat up the food. Someone had given us a pot of peas and rice. So, once we had gathered some wood, the food would be heated and the class would get to enjoy that inviting pot of food.

Well, while we were outside, one of the kids hit me with a switch. (In case you are too young to know what that is, it's a branch from a small tree or bush.) I was not one to suffer injustice. So, I voiced my disapproval and we started an argument. I think that boy would have beaten me up, if my sister hadn't helped me out. As it were, we beat him. This kind of thing was not a regular occurrence. Although, I was very vocal and never backed down from anybody.

Like church, school was not optional. We had to attend school. If our shoes were old and the soles were leaving the shoes, my parents would use wire to attach the soles back onto our shoes.

As fate would have it, I only went to school up to the seventh grade. I did not, however, complete the seventh grade. I only went for about 2 weeks. But never the less, I was always an avid reader.

While school was important, I saw the struggles that my family was enduring and I wanted to help. So, I dropped out of school in order to earn money to help my family. My heart always wanted to help those in need, and my family was in need.

What I learned from that point on was learned from life and from constantly reading everything. That combined with the training that I received from my parents gave me a rich "common sense" education. Combining that with faith in God and the willingness to work has helped me to move mountains.

I would not, however, recommend dropping out of school to anyone. You would miss out on the structure and valuable knowledge that you can pull from to help you move forward with your life. Get all of the education you can get. Education gives you choices. Besides, we live in a different time now than when I was growing up. Life is more complex today. You want to get all the help you can get in this world to help insure that you succeed. Education helps.

2

BUILDING A FAMILY

A Perfect Match

In my teen-age years, the place where the young people loved to hang out was *Bob Nichols*. Well, it wasn't actually a place; it was an event featuring *Bob Nichols*. *Bob Nichols* was actually a disc jockey. He worked at radio station WPAL in Charleston, South Carolina. He came to Brown's Ferry School, from time to time and there would be a dance. *Bob Nichols* played the equivalent of disco music for our era. People would pay to enter. I was around 13 or 14 years old. I loved dancing and boy could I dance up a storm. I remember dancing to the music of artists like Wilson Pickett and Chuck Berry - good music. That was entertainment, and I was thoroughly entertained. We enjoyed ourselves.

As I was enjoying my teen-age years, one day, while walking to one of my aunts' house, I met a handsome young man driving a beautiful car. He was my aunt's nephew, on his mother's side. We began to talk. Week after week, we talked. My daddy suspected something and warned, "I hope you are not seeing nobody called 'your boyfriend.' This can't happen because you are too young to have a boyfriend."

I was 15 years old. And you know how siblings are. They love to blackmail you when something juicy is going on, "If you don't give me something, I'll sure tell on you." You know I did pay up, because I did sneak around and see him, repeatedly. Even at the age of 15, I still kept seeing him.

Now, we didn't have any money. So, I would bribe my siblings with a piece of candy or food or some kind of treat. My father didn't like it very much, but after a while, he would give us a break so we could talk to each other. Today, we are still talking.

In my late teens, I moved to New York to live with one of my brothers, but I didn't like it very much and I missed my family. I only stayed for about a year. Living in New York at first was okay, but I really missed my family. So, I came back home in December of 1961.

On January 27, 1962, I married the most handsome guy there was. It was that same young man I started talking to at age 15. He was 22 years old and I was 19. We planned that wedding in one month.

Oh how I remember the year 1962. In those days, in my community, when you got married, you lived in the family house. So, we lived with my husband's family. We had one room to ourselves.

I remember the Saturday of the wedding. Now, we got married outside in the yard. That was normal back then. The ceremony was in the front yard. Herbert, the groom, wore a black and white tuxedo, which he rented. He looked so sharp and handsome. I wore a white and blue dress. The pastor said, "until death do you part." That was it – a new beginning.

Back then, we didn't have formal invitations. Invitation went by word of mouth. If you heard about it, you could consider yourself invited. People came from all over the community and they brought all kinds of food and cake. It was a feast. A big pan of cake was passed out in the yard among the people who came. And each person took a piece of cake until it was gone. A reserved table was set up for the bride and groom, their immediate family and the bridal party. The people at the reserved table were served. The others either went up to the kitchen or ate some of the cake that was passed around.

One of the older neighbors said to us, "I'll drive you up to the place of stay." He added, "I want y'all to remember I took y'all to your place of stay." He was high and drinking. In fact, he drove his car into the ditch and then he said, "You will remember this happened on your wedding day." He was really a joking kind of guy. He is now gone on to live with God.

When we got married, Herbert was making about $40.00 a week. No matter how hard the times got, however, we never slept in the dark. My family always had clothes to wear and food to eat. Out of the little bit of money he made, we made ends meet. I always worked, from the time I was a child. I worked and raised my babies at the same time. Family members helped with babysitting needs.

Many people in the surrounding communities planted vegetable gardens. So, you very often had fresh home grown vegetables. My husband and I had a garden. Some of what our garden included were cabbage and sweet potatoes. We also planted tobacco and cucumber. These were things you took to the market to sell. We started planting crops about 2-3 years into our marriage and continued for years. The land was family property which we had permission to use.

Our marriage has been a very good marriage. I believe that my father contributed to this. He taught his daughters that "You are not the man." Early on, I remember one night my husband and I got into an argument. My father sat over in the corner and said, "Herbert, you are the man." I thank my parents today, because if they had taken side with me, I would probably be somewhere else today with no husband to help me. I was stubborn and opinionated. In a marriage, you have to learn how to make peace. You can't always have things your way.

Today, I am grateful to my father for his advice because my marriage is strong. I also thank God for my beloved husband who has supported my every endeavor. So many times I have said, "We don't have much but we have each other." And after 55 years, we are still laughing and talking. And yes, we still fuss a little bit too. In fact, sometimes we sound just like little children. I am glad my father allowed us to talk. We seem to have made a perfect match.

As it turns out, we are still together and we have 2 girls, 5 boys, 13 grandchildren and 9 great grandchildren.

As I look over my life, I must acknowledge that God has really blessed me.

Like Mother, Like Children

Unlike me, all of my children finished high school. I thank God for my children. While I didn't have the opportunity to do so, I am so happy my children took advantage of getting a good education. And they have grown into loving, caring, responsible adults. I am proud to have them as my children.

Our oldest son, Michael, went to college, but he did not finish. He did, however, find work at the local steel mill. The mill later closed. He is now working for an oil company. He also works as a football coach at the new high school – Carver's Bay High School.

Andrew, our second son, whom we nicknamed Andy, went in the United States Army after high school. Afterwards, he spent many years living in New York. But eventually, he ended up moving back home to South Carolina. Health issues have made him unable to work.

Our third child is also a male. His name is Mark. He is very quiet and very concerned about people. His hard work has earned him accomplishments in several areas. He has multiple degrees. He went into the U.S.

Army for 4 years. Then, he went to college for 4 years and earned a bachelor's degree in Business Administration.

Afterwards, he went to work at the steel mill. He worked and built a house for himself on the river front, near the Black River. When the steel mill closed, he had saved enough money to continue on with his education. So, he did. He has, since, graduated from radiology training and he has received his Master's Degree as an RN.

Mark is now working at the Williamsburg Mental Health Department. He volunteered part-time at an assisted living facility, in the area, while he was in school and he continues to do so, today. And he volunteers in the community at health fairs and church events when needed. He also works part-time at the Georgetown Hospital.

Someone said to me one day, "You and all of your children are the most volunteering family I have ever known." It is a good thing to volunteer in the community. It is called "giving back."

My oldest daughter, Michelle, is very easy going. When she was in high school, she enjoyed the nursing class and did very well in it. She loved going along with the teacher when she had a class where she had to speak about nursing. Michelle even went to college with the intention of becoming a nurse.

Then one day Michelle called and said, "I am on my way home as soon as I get enough money." She didn't like it at the school. I said, "Lord, Girl, you don't know what you are doing. Education is the way out." But she came home and got a job at a nursing home. She worked for about a year and came to me one day and said she was going to New York to visit her brother, Andy, for a week. That week ended 17 years later.

Michelle has, since, expressed regret at not completing college. While she was thinking about going back to college, someone called and offered me a job. I laughed and told her that I would volunteer but I couldn't work 8 hours a day. Then, I told her about my daughter, Michelle. Michelle took that job in health care. I told Michelle that it is good to work hard and do well. Be honest and truthful, and things will work out for you.

Things worked out well. Michelle has worked diligently. She has since gotten an opportunity to work with special needs children and she loves it.

Michelle also loves to cook and feed the family. What a great cook she is! Maybe, one day she will have a restaurant - another way of caring for people.

Tranja is our youngest daughter. She is a very expressive and opinionated person; she knows what she wants. And even as a baby, she always loved people.

As a little girl, Tranja was very smart in school. She was also committed to her goals. This was very evident when she wanted to be a majorette. She worked very hard and did not stop until she became an accomplished majorette. I was very proud of her.

Not only was she a great majorette, but she always made good grades. When she was in the 10th grade, however, she had a bit of a challenge. She got pregnant. Never the less, Tranja did not let that stop her. The baby was born and she continued in high school. She graduated along with her class.

Tranja had a beautiful baby boy. My husband and I, along with my other children helped in raising him. In fact, my husband and I, in time, legally adopted Tranja's baby. We wanted her to be able to focus on her education and get herself together.

About a year prior to Tranja's pregnancy, I was interviewed for an article on the subject of teen pregnancy. I spoke out against teen pregnancy. I felt that the young ladies should focus on getting an education and become more informed before having children. They have their whole life ahead. The article was later printed in the newspaper. When Tranja got pregnant, I said, "Satan, you are a good liar. You try to shame me, but I will get over this one." (Just because you live close to God, it doesn't mean you won't have serious incidents in your life.) I haven't changed my mind.

After finishing high school, Tranja went on to college. She completed 2 years in Human Services and Accounting and she always worked while she was in school. Now, she is working at the paper mill in Georgetown.

She is now divorced, but owns her own home and is still working and doing well. She has a daughter who is now an adult. We'll talk about her later. She's one of the miracles in my life.

When my fourth son was born, we named him Herbert, after his father. My older sons were upset about his name. They said, "Mama, that's an old man's name." For a year or so, they would only call him "the baby." And my daughter Tranja complained that if Herbert wasn't born, she would've been the baby. But, eventually, they all mellowed out. I worked and my mother babysat Herbert - affectionately called Herbie.

When he was a toddler, there was a period of time when Herbie did not want to eat. Since he didn't want to eat, I took him to the doctor. The doctor told me, "When he gets ready, he will eat."

At that same time, Michael, my oldest son, was in college. Once, when he came home he said to Herbie,

"Come on Herbie. My name is 'Big Mouth' and you're name is 'Little Big Mouth' and when I eat you eat." Herbie started eating and is still eating. He looks like he enjoys eating. He has gotten to be my largest son. In fact he went to college for cooking. And he does catering for different occasions.

I kept Herbie in church with me, when he was a baby. Where ever I went, he was there. As a teen-ager and young adult, every meeting I attended he was there. He helped to pass out flyers for various projects that I worked on and helped with publicity as well as other tasks. And he helped with training for the Georgetown County Diabetes CORE Group.

As I mentioned earlier, we adopted one of our grandsons - Tranja's son, Joshua. Josh for short. We raised him as our own. He also graduated high school and went to college. Josh was very athletic. In fact, he was the captain of the football team in high school.

My husband and I spent a lot of money to send Josh to college. There were times when we had to show him tough love. He had decided, after a while, that he didn't want to continue in college. My grandson had the audacity to say that he went to college because *we* wanted him to go. So, we backed off. We said to him, "Son, you are on your own. We have done what we could for you."

When my grandson found out that you had to have an education for most jobs, he went back to school. We let him pay for his own college education and he made it on his own. He is a college graduate.

For a short time, he gave us a stir. Once, when he was in high school, I received a call from the school regarding his behavior. So, I went to the school. When I got there, they told me that he had been in the bathroom with some other guys and that they were about to drink Grey Goose liquor. I called my daughter, Tranja. She beat him and taught him a lesson he will never forget. In fact, I had to pull her off of him.

He has told other family members that his grandmother is a strong woman. "My grandmother had to pull Mama off me," he recounts the story.

Josh has never revealed where he and his friends got that liquor. Afterwards, we sent him to a drug abuse center to see if he was participating or experimenting with other drugs. He came home one evening and said, "I am not a drug abuser. I don't need to be in that class." "You are going to stay," was our reply.

Now, Josh says that going to that class was a good experience for him. When he attended that class, he saw firsthand what could happen, if he was into drinking and drugs. He heard and saw things he would never have heard or seen, otherwise. So today, he is thankful and I am thankful for what transpired.

All of my children had very happy days just like my childhood. We laughed a lot. They laughed a lot. I taught them that education is the most important thing you can get. It opens up the doors to opportunities in your life. They have taken that advice to heart and have built successful lives and they care about helping people. And like I was with my siblings, they are very close and very respectful.

3

Answering the Call

Growing up, my family was Baptist, but the girls were raised to follow their husbands. So, when I got married, I didn't lose any time in joining my husband's church. I was Baptist and he was Methodist. My father said, "If you pull cover with him, then you should be in the same church." So, we began our life together at the same church – Nazareth AME Church in the Choppee Section of Georgetown County, South Carolina.

I went to church, but I wasn't saved. I was young and not concerned about that. When you are young, you think you have all of the time in the world.

One night, in the early 70's, while on the way to church, the minister was talking to me, in the car, about living for the Lord. I told him, "Some people say they are too young." His reply was, "You are never too young."

I began working at Winyah Nursing home in 1973. That job lasted for about 4 years.

It was there, at Winyah Nursing Home, that I, one day, met a 90 year old woman. She said to me, "Do you know who Jesus is?" I said, "Yes." She said, "If he comes for you right now, will you be ready?" I stood quietly. She said, "You couldn't answer."

Afterwards, I began to really think about what she said. As a little girl, my parents taught us about who Jesus is and about his love for us. But I wasn't giving it much serious consideration. I was basically a "good person."

I, also, met a young man at Winyah Nursing Home who was "in the Word." One morning, that young man had a message for me. He said to me, "Mrs. Linnen, you shouldn't be wearing that dress and *dancing* around." (He thought my dress was too short.) He said to me, "God can use you because you love people and they listen when you talk. God needs you." My reply was, "I am not ready, yet."

Well, one night while I was out clubbing, I looked at myself in the mirror on the wall and I suddenly came to the realization that I did not need to be there. It was at that point that I started thinking about my soul.

About 3 years after that conversation with the minister in the car on the way to church, on the third Friday night in August of 1973, as the minister was preaching, "Drink from the Living Water," I found myself praising God, and I just couldn't stop! Everything looked different to me. It seemed like my eyes became so clear. I began to pray and fast, immediately, that night, that the Lord would get the glory out of my soul.

You know, I used to smoke cigarettes, drink beer, and I loved to party. My husband and I, we partied together. We had a great time at *Bob Nichols* and other clubs. Of course, I was always a better dancer than he was. But I'll always remember the night I gave my life to Jesus – the 3rd Friday in August of 1973. I gave my life to Jesus and started to live and dance for him. It didn't make life easy, but it was just the joy of knowing who you are and who you belong to. Nothing could bring that joy, but Jesus.

From that point on, God began to give me things to do in helping people. I was looking for work one day. A young lady said to me, "We are looking for volunteers to assist people with reading. Are you interested?" That sounded good to me because I loved helping people. So, I said, "Yes."

Well, I worked for close to a year as a volunteer. Then, that volunteer job turned into a paying job. That job was with Waccamaw Economic Opportunity Council (EOC). I had a job helping people and I loved it. I was there for about 5 years, until funding ran out.

As I think back, I remember an incident at Georgetown Laundry. Incidentally, I worked there twice. While I was there, I was witnessing about the Goodness of God. The supervisor said to me one day that he was a man not "in the Word." I didn't hold it against him. But he said to me, "Don't do that in here! Take it on the outside." So I said, "Sir, I can go out here." And I quit. I had no job; no money. I went home. I left that job, but I stayed with God.

The older brothers in the church along with the older mothers taught the young people God's way. Over the years, I have worked in many capacities in my church. I listened and learned and I went to work in the church.

My work in the church began as an usher, greeting people as they came into the church. Later, I also joined the choir. It's been over 43 years and I still sing in the choir. Additionally, I also taught Sunday School at our church and I worked as health director for the 32 churches of our district for 16 years.

In the AME church, we have an office called *class leader*. My class leader died and I was elected as the class leader for my class - Class No. 1. This was many years ago and I am still class leader.

For a total of 19 years, I have been a missionary. As a missionary of my church, I have seen many things and helped many people. I stood by many people's bed side and sang as they crossed over. I was president for 8 years which is the maximum number of years one is allowed to serve as president. After a year out of office, I was voted back in.

I went into many jails and prison camps with the missionaries to encourage people not to give up. In my service as a missionary, I've seen many young people destroy themselves with drugs and alcohol. In hospitals, I visited many people. Some couldn't move even their hands. I thank God for the opportunities He gave me to visit and provide comfort for those in need.

It has been over 40 years since I chose to give my life to Jesus, and I am still enjoying Jesus. He keeps me walking with faith. The doors that have been opened and the favors he has shown me with people are unbelievable. God has put me in places and allowed me to do things that I would never have been able to do without him. And He's brought me out of places I could never have found my way out of.

I thank God for His leadership in my life. I laugh sometimes when I think about the dance floor and the partying. I always wanted people to have a good time. But as you know, when you are young sometimes that is all you think about. Well, I am still having a good time with Jesus.

4

A WILLING WORKER

Over the years, I have worked a variety of different jobs. Many of them were jobs working with impoverished people in the community. My jobs gave me the opportunity to work with the young and the old. And I have learned a lot about dealing with people. Those various jobs have helped me to prepare for the work that I do with diabetes. I've had many challenges and pitfalls along the way, but they all just made me stronger.

In my adult life, I have had many jobs. Some of my jobs included operating a knitting machine at a factory in

Andrews, working at the Georgetown Laundry(twice), Winyah Nursing Home, Department of Youth Services, Waccamaw EOC (twice), and the paper mill.

I remember working at a factory in Andrews, S.C. - Grove Shipyard. It was a job wherein I operated a knitting machine. My job was to knit the material before it was laundered. Well, it was about 3:00 in the afternoon, one day, when I started crying. The problem? I wanted to go home. (I don't remember why.) The manager asked me, "You want to go home?" I answered, "Yes." And that was it for me. I didn't go back, after that. This was the early 60s and I had been working there for 2 years. That was enough for me.

Several years later, still in the 60s, I got a job planting trees for the International Paper Company. I worked out in the woods. Well, it was a job. And we made very good money for that time.

It was in the early 80s that I worked for the Department of Youth Services. My responsibility was to complete the proper paperwork on the young people after they had been arrested. Then, I would try to help them find a parent or guardian to come to get them and take them home, so that they did not have to spend the night in the jail house.

If they were arrested for a minor offense, they could be released to a parent or guardian. Sometimes, I sat with the young people and waited for their parents until the wee hours of the night. If no one came to get them, they went to lock up.

Regardless of whether a parent or guardian came to get them, I would turn the paper work in to the Department of Youth Services to be handled by someone else. They, then, took the paperwork and handled it with the sheriff's department and the courts.

I was never too proud to hold any job that produced something positive. I was always willing to work. Once, when I was looking for a job, I walked into a place of employment and spotted a lady down the hall. I told her that I was looking for a job. This was 1973. She said, "We are looking for someone, if you want this kind of work." I told her, "I will work wherever there is a job; just give me a chance." A few weeks later, I was hired. I left that job in 1977. But that lady and I remained friends until she passed away in 2017. In fact, I spoke at her funeral. I had met a friend for life. That job was with Winyah Nursing Home.

At Winyah Nursing Home, I did housekeeping; I cleaned the patients' rooms. But sometimes, the patients and I would just talk. I would assist the patients with different things, and let the nurses know what the patients needed from them - things that I could not do. One young lady that worked there, later said to me, "Mrs. Linnen, you were good to work with, but we were glad when you left because you caused us to work too hard."

In 1982, I returned to work at Waccamaw EOC. I knew someone who worked there. She told me about a job opening. I applied and I was hired. This was my second time working at Waccamaw EOC and I remained at Waccamaw until 2002 doing community outreach work.

While working with Waccamaw EOC, I traveled throughout the three counties of Georgetown, Horry and Williamsburg, to work with impoverished families. I was glad to be able to help. And as I worked, I sent up prayers for the people. I was not only helping people, but I was, unknowingly, building relationships that would later benefit even more people.

As I think back, sometimes I tried to help people and ended up in trouble. There was one man who I recommended for a job at Waccamaw EOC, where I was working at the time. Well, there was a report of an incident (Let's just leave it at that.) involving that man and a client, and I wound up having to go to court because I recommended him.

The client filed a complaint and my job, Waccamaw EOC, was being sued by the client because of the reported incident. It took a while (about 2-3 years) before the case went to court. My supervisor, another associate and I were questioned extensively. Because I recommended the man, my employer thought that I knew things about him that I really did not know.

I had to answer a lot of questions. In fact, one day, the lawyer for my company called me at work and asked me to come to his office so that he could take a deposition. He kept me at his office until 10 o'clock at night. He kept going over a list questions he thought that the other lawyer was going to ask. During the time leading up to the court date, in addition to answering questions, the lawyer also told me things that he thought the other lawyer was going to say; he would try to say things about me that were really not true. And he advised me to be prepared.

This was a serious time. Things did not look good for a while. When we finally went to court, we were only there one day. I was sitting in the courtroom next to the lawyer for Waccamaw EOC when he told me that the case was over. Then, the judge announced it to the courtroom. It turns out that the insurance company had settled. So we never went to trial. Also, the accused employee was not convicted of any crime stemming from this reported incident.

"God you done it for me again," was all I could say. I was there because I tried to help someone. I thank so many people for their support and concern during that time. I kept a good attitude about it all.

As I write this, I recall going into my office, at Waccamaw EOC one day, and before I got out of the car good, I saw this lady who worked in the next office. I said to her, "Good morning." She replied, "What is good about it?" I told her, "You are alive!" She was very angry. I never could figure out why she was so angry. She was doing better than our clients were doing.

Anger leads to high blood pressure and stress. I learned as a little girl that a smile takes fewer muscles, but when you are angry and all frowned up, all of your muscles are working. "A good attitude determines your altitude," I always say. I am going to keep a good attitude.

5

COMMUNITY

Helping people was always something that I enjoyed. Over the years, I have gotten involved in community activities over and over. Where ever I saw a need, I organized groups and initiated various projects within my community.

The rural community is known for poverty. For many people, even the bare necessities can be an issue. Years ago, I facilitated the community coming together and forming the *Helping Hands Club*. The group helped people to pay their light bills, medical bills and other essentials.

Assistance included budgeting tips, training and monetary donations. It was a very successful initiative. We laughed at ourselves on the kick off day because we cooked the food and turned around and bought the food from each other.

We felt that it was important to be organized. So, we had a president, treasurer, and a few board members. We elected these ladies to work in their own communities and use their own people. People found out about the service by word of mouth. Community members volunteered and taught as needed.

I believe that it was all in God's plan. We got together and did fundraisings so people could live more comfortable lives. To much is given; much is expected.

We also had a program where we worked on homes of the senior citizens. People in their own communities can come together and assist each other with many needs. It builds the community and it builds people's confidence in each other. It is a win-win situation. The overall community gains and the individual residents gain. The contributors feel good and the beneficiaries are better off. It is also my continuous hope and prayer that individuals and families will have increased financial growth and improved living conditions.

One thing that I prayed so hard about was a project where we were working on the home of a family in the Choppee community. We were renovating the home. The rain came before we finished. It was a praying time because everything we tried to do the Devil would hinder us. But Satan had to step back. Our prayers prevailed.

The people had to move out of their house, temporarily. They were housed in a nearby building which was empty. They were allowed to stay on the downstairs floor until the work was done on their home. There was no charge to them for the accommodations.

I did a lot of community work through my church. We initiated projects through the Missionary Society of Nazareth AME Church. The very first African Banquet was done under my leadership of the missionaries. We shared education about African culture. The young people of our church performed an African dance at the banquet. Everyone was excited to learn information about their heritage. The African Banquet was just one of the many fundraisers of our missionary department.

Another thing that our missionaries did was put on a program to help buy a bus. We needed transportation to go to different places for the church. This missionary program was called "Missionaries of the Year." We did an education project based on the contiguous 48 states of the U.S. We had 48 ladies, each representing one the 48 States. And each missionary shared information about the health disparities of the state she represented. It was very educational.

My work over the years, especially my community outreach work, and various community activities caused me to travel to areas beyond my local communities. Sometimes it got very challenging. I recall coming from Columbia, S.C. one night. The wheels on the car started making all kinds of noises, and I was alone. I kept on driving, slowly however, because I was about three miles from home. My home was in the rural community of Dunbar. I made it home safely. To God, be the glory. If it had happened farther away from home, I would have been in trouble. Those were some long, dark, desolate roads.

As I think back, in the 70's people were totally different from the way they are today. I would not try that now because people have changed. I think it's a lot more dangerous today, to be out here on those long dark roads, in the middle of the night. Because this generation is totally different; and not in a good way.

On another occasion, while I was working for Waccamaw EOC, I had an incident with my car. I was returning from working in the Pee Dee community when the lights on the car started blinking. Then they went out. So, I pulled over to the side. When nothing was coming, I would drive slowly. When I saw a light down the road, again, I pulled to the side. I did this stop and start practice until I, eventually, arrived home.

I kept going because I was thinking that it would be 12:00 AM before they would start looking for me.

You might wonder why I took those risks. I chose to work and attend meetings - anything to be on top for the communities with which I worked. I worked long hours - as long as it took to win the community's confidence and provide help. I worked out of my car for years while working with Waccamaw EOC. I had my clients' best interest at heart and I wanted to see them with a better life.

I am so glad for the training that I received while working for Waccamaw EOC and working in the communities. The skills that I learned are valuable in working with people anywhere.

Sometimes, when I think about it, I just laugh. I have been the chairperson of many boards. Once, I even got fired (smile) from one of them. Something was not right, and I knew it. Well, they fired me because I told them I disagreed. You know, they had the nerve to still want me to serve on the board as a member? My answer to them was, "You don't trust me and I don't trust you." I added, "But as long as the facts are present, the truth is what I'll stand for."

6

TAKING A STAND

In the 90s, drugs were very much on the rise in the communities where I lived and worked. So, I called a meeting and met with the neighboring communities. I told them that we could not let drugs take over our communities. At that meeting, we decided to do a march.

I went to my church and told them that we as a community are going to march against the drugs in our community. The march was going to take place from Mt. Olive Baptist Church to the Dunbar Bridge. This bridge connects the communities of Dunbar and Choppee, which are separated by the Black River.

Well, the news got out that there was going to be a march against drugs. Then, I was in my office one day and a young lady came in and said to me, "Mrs. Linnen, how are you?" "I am very good and very fine," I replied. The young lady, then, said, "No, you are not, because I was in the washer last night and I heard some talk." She went on to explain, "A man said he got an Uzi gun for a Florene Linnen for stopping his sale." I told her, "Go back and tell him I got one too that is much bigger than his Uzi, 'cause I got Jesus." And I said, most emphatically, "There will be a march!"

The word got out that these folks were saying that if they couldn't get me, they would get my children. So, I started taking precautions. I would call the school to make sure that my kids and grandkids got on the bus. I would take them to the bus and I would meet them at the bus stop at the end of the day. I never told the children what was going on.

That Saturday morning when it was time for the march, we had a pastor from Nazareth AME church, government officials from Georgetown and Santee along with some people from the communities. That night, one place - a hole in the wall club - went up in fire. Of course, people were thinking that I had something to do with it, but I didn't. That is not how I operate.

We had a park in the Choppee community called Rocky Point Park. When we were young adults, Rocky Point Park was part of our entertainment. It was right on the Black River. The Lord laid it on my heart to bring the communities and churches together for a day to unite at Rocky Point Park.

I contacted the missionaries from three churches. We had government officials and the sheriff's department to talk about drugs and what to look for in our children's rooms or cars. Several health agencies were also present. We were united that day with pastors, missionaries and residents from the communities coming together. The participation was awesome!

After years of tree growth and vines, the Rocky Point Park was cleaned up by the communities. It was a happy day. Due to lack of use, however, years later the Rocky Point Park was closed.

The communities have supported me in many things. I have been threatened because I stand against some things. I have been fired for standing for the truth. I have been involved in a lawsuit and faced the possibility of having my character attacked as a result of trying to be helpful. But God has shown me favor. People have always been my heart. And I will always help in any way that I can. I refuse to allow fear to stop me. It might make me a little nervous, but I will always stand on faith.

7

MIRACLES IN MY LIFE

I am extremely grateful for the life I've had and all of the many blessings I have received, especially the miracles in my life. My life has been an amazing journey. I would go so far as to say that it has been miraculous.

A Miracle at my Door

One of the miracles in my life is my son, Andy. He became very sick very suddenly and his wife took him to the hospital in Georgetown. The health professionals at the hospital sent Andy back home. In that same day, we (I had returned home by then.) took him right back to the hospital.

Then, his doctor said, "Mrs. Linnen, I'll be honest with the family. We will transport him to MUSC and it's going to go straight downhill." In addition, we were told, "He is going to be paralyzed."

These were unbelievable words to hear. We were told that he would have a tracheal tube in his throat and he would go back to a baby-like state. The doctor said that all we could do was give him much love and keep talking to him. By giving him much support, maybe he would be okay.

We, immediately, had Andy transferred to Medical University of South Carolina (MUSC) in Charleston, S.C. Andy was diagnosed with Guillain-Barré Syndrome (GBS). He got it from a flu shot. Ironically, the thing that was supposed to save his life nearly killed him. We were told that his condition could go either way. He could get better; he could get worse.

According to the Centers for Disease Control and Prevention, approximately 3,000 to 6,000 people develop GBS each year whether or not they receive a vaccination.

Well, he was hospitalized and unable to move a muscle for months. His body was completely paralyzed. As it turned out, while he could not move a muscle, he was able to hear. (Of course, that means he could hear the good as well as the bad. So, watch what you say around sick people.) Loving him and talking to him mattered. That was his life line.

Andy was a fighter. Even when he was on the life support machine, he was still able to move his eyes. And he heard everything that was said.

It was a long drive from Georgetown to MUSC in Charleston. But I wanted to keep up with Andy's recovery. So, I went there repeatedly. One morning I got up and I said I wasn't going to see Andy that day. I started praying for him, instead. The next thing I realized, I was crying. It was just a mother's response in the moment. I cried and cried until God gave me more strength and faith to stop crying. My daughter, Tranja, came over and said, "Oh, Mama, what's the matter? Is Andy dead?" I was so glad that I had cried. It was such a relief. I said to my daughter, "No, he is not dead. It is just a mother's love for her child."

We thank the Good Lord for Andy; and also for the doctors and the nurses at MUSC, for the care that they gave Andy. His wife, Lisa, did not leave the hospital until he recovered. She slept there. She had clothes with her and she bathed and changed her clothes in the hospital. She stayed right by his side for all of those months.

Then, one day, I was in my house and I heard a knock on the door. I walked over and opened the door. There was Andy standing at my door grinning away. Look at the way God worked in his life. God brought a miracle to my door!

Flying by Faith

My third son, Mark, was in an accident in Texas. We received the call and my husband and I discussed it. Afterwards, my husband told me to go on the plane and he would drive out there afterwards and see what's going on. This was the first time I had ever ridden on a plane. I said, "I am going Lord, but please travel with me."

The way the events unfolded was nothing less than miraculous. In Myrtle Beach, I boarded the plane for Texas. When I got on the plane, there was this young man (school age) that I sat next to. He saw that I was having trouble buckling my seat belt. So, he buckled it for me. He informed me of various things that I didn't know, but should be made aware of.

During the conversation, I found out that he was heading to a class reunion. He was a very well-mannered young man. I told him about my son's accident in Texas. He said, "Mrs. Linnen, that's where I am going. You don't want to go there, but I am going to call you a taxi cab." Because I knew nothing about traveling, he was going to speak to the cab and tell him where to take me. He cautioned me that these cabs will ride you around and charge you so much money because you don't know the area.

The taxi driver who picked me up lived in a motel with his family. He found me a room in the same motel. Then, the same taxi driver drove me out to the hospital where my son was. He took good care of me.

My son was in the hospital for a few days. And, then, Mark and I came back to South Carolina on the Greyhound bus. My husband drove back home, alone. Herbert, my husband, and Mark drove back to Texas about three weeks later to get Mark's belongings out his car, which had been towed to a storage area.

I was clueless about traveling, but by the grace of God, I was well taken care of by that taxi driver and the young man whom I met on the plane. And, my son was not fatally injured. For me, it was nothing less than miraculous. To God be the glory.

Shakema

My granddaughter, Shakema, was nine months old when she started being sick. We came in from church one night and Tranja, her mother, said to me, "The baby is sick." Shakema was as limp as a piece of cloth. We took her to the local hospital in Georgetown. They, right away, took her to MUSC in Charleston via medivac.

Shakema was having 27 to 30 seizures per day. The doctors said that when she got to be 5 years old, they would do surgery. My granddaughter had a cyst on the brain. For 4 more years, she would be having 27 to 30 seizures per day. The doctors even thought, at one point, that she could not hear. This was a job for Jesus and we prayed continuously.

At 5 years of age, Shakema had the cyst removed. After surgery, she woke up and said to the doctor, "What's up, boy?" She was used to seeing doctors, but she never called them "doctor." The doctors had said that after surgery, her head would be swollen and her eyes would be swollen. They said that it would be a while before we could even talk to her.

Well, we were all very pleased that the doctors' predictions were incorrect. Shakema did not have the expected swelling. She spoke immediately and she could hear. Needless to say, the doctors were very pleased with the surgery. After the surgery, the seizures were greatly reduced.

As time went on, she was always sick and she was always in and out of school. Her mother, father and I stuck with her. Keema, as we have come to call her, was in and out of the hospital until she was about 18 years old.

When she started school, we had many battles with the teachers. They wanted to brand her as retarded and unable to learn. We had to attend school board meetings, repeatedly. But she went through regular public school and passed every year.

We had to make many trips to the school and attend many meetings. After all the years of fighting to keep her in school and not be labeled as unable to function, they had the nerve to try to deny her the right to march at graduation from middle school. They felt that she would throw off the timing of the other students as they marched. Should she not be allowed to march because she had trouble with rhythm? We could not accept that. Through prayer and perseverance and a lot of love and care, she completed and marched.

My advice to all parents and grandparents: look out for your children. Labeling your child might get you a few dollars in your pocket, but it might not be beneficial for the child in the long run. Nurture their development and stand up for them.

Keema was so proud when she completed middle school and high school. And yes, she marched.

When she completed high school, we contemplated sending her to college. I told my granddaughter what I have told my children, that she needs an education in order to be successful in society.

My family discussed it and we decided that it would not be the best thing for her to go to college because she is so nice and people are so cruel. We did not want to put her in a situation where people could take advantage of her. She requires some supervision.

Keema attends J.O.Y. School University in Pawley's Island, South Carolina. J.O.Y. School University caters to adults over 21 who have a variety of abilities. Some of the students have jobs. Here Keema gets to participate in various activities that help her to retain what she has already learned as well as share social time with others. She loves the arts, computers and singing in the choir at church.

Shakema has come a long way from 27-30 seizures per day. "The effectual and fervent prayer of a righteous man availeth much." Prayer, courage, hard work and love have saved her life and given her a chance to be a functioning part of society and spread her love everywhere she goes. She is a loving young lady and a walking miracle. Oh Bless the Lord for his mercy and his grace.

Surviving Cancer

Cancer is what most of my family died of. My father suffered with cancer for 6 years. His faith was very strong all the way to the end. The doctor told my father he would live six months; my father lived six years. He was a great man of faith. In fact when the doctor said he would live 6 months, my father said, "God didn't say that." (Smile) I remember the morning when the doctor said he would be with the Lord in a few minutes. My father said, "Come here children. I just want to put my head on your shoulders. And don't cry for me because you all have done all you could for me." Silas Jackson was a man of God.

My mother was diagnosed with liver cancer at the age of 85. We had taken her on a vacation to visit one of her children. She had an exam before we went on the trip and the results were good. When we returned from our trip, she became ill. We took her to the doctor again and he immediately sent her to the hospital in Georgetown for tests.

The first day at the hospital they said her sugar was out of control. For 3 days, they ran tests on her. On the third day, the doctor sent for the children. What he told us was very shocking. The doctor said, "I don't know where it came from, but she has cancer throughout her body." He followed that announcement with, "Your mother will only live three months." They had found that she had liver cancer.

The doctor apologized because they had checked her out before she went on the trip and did not find anything. My mother took it very well. She said, "I hear you doctor. If I live here to be an 85 year-old lady and don't think I am going to die, oh what a shame."

My mother began making preparations for her death. She prepared us well. She listed all the people she wanted on her obituary. Then, she told me, "Even though the house is in your name, I want your daughter to have the house." She was talking about Michelle who was paying rent at the time and she also had a son. In three months, my mother was gone.

My mother had a Holy Ghost funeral. It was sad and at the same time joyous.

It is very important that we have regular checkups. As we can see with my mother, sometimes they miss the problem. But much of the time they make an accurate diagnosis. Additionally, it is very important that we women have a mammogram, regularly. Early detection could save your life.

Well, once again, it was time for my annual mammogram. The year was 2004. I was planning to retire that year from MUSC REACH 2010. That was my plan, but before I could retire, I found myself diagnosed with breast cancer. At this point, I had been an advocate of diabetes care, and working with the Diabetes CORE Group for 7 years. I had retired form Waccamaw EOC in 2002.

Leaving my home that morning, going to the doctor for my annual mammogram was something I always did. When I got there, I said to the doctor jokingly, "Well, doctor, whatever we have to do, let's do it. If you find anything, take it off." Little did I know that he would find a tumor.

I went back to work forgetting all about the examination. At that time, I was working in the Andrews area in connection with diabetes with MUSC REACH 2010. When I came home from work one day, I received a message from my family that my supervisor was trying to reach me. I called my supervisor and she said that the doctor was trying to reach me. (I did not have a cellphone.)

Immediately, I called the doctor. He wanted me to come in for the feedback from my mammogram. So, I set up an appointment. When I arrived at my appointment, the doctor said, "You have cancer in the right breast." Again I said, "Whatever has to be done, let's do it."

At first, I felt very sad. Simply, hearing the word "cancer" made me very upset. Then, it came to me: "Trust God."

When you get up in the morning you trust God that things are going to work out for you. I gave my life to God a long time ago. Technology is advancing every day for early detection of illnesses. And for what technology cannot do, I have learned to depend on God. My children were very sad about the situation. I told them to cheer up because I was in God's hands.

I went into the hospital early in 2004. My pastor, my friends, my sister Rose, my husband and my supervisor from MUSC REACH 2010 were there.
The doctor performed a lumpectomy.

The operation was a success. Two months later, I started radiation treatment. For a while, I did well while working and taking my scheduled treatments. After about 6-8 weeks, I began getting so tired and worn out.

I began to get sick while I was working. I really loved my job, but I wanted to quit.

After treatment one day, I started feeling very tired and nauseated. I just got sick. And I said, "Lord, I don't feel like continuing on, but I need to endure until my treatment is over. I just don't know. One thing I do know is you are in charge. So, now I will let my supervisor know how I am feeling."

So, I went into her office and let it all out. "I can't make it any more." My supervisor listened to me very intently. Then, she took her time, crossed her legs and replied, "And what are you going to do - go home and die? Because that is what will happen to you. You will give up." I thought about what she said. And then I exclaimed, "Oh, no! I am not going home to die!"

She, then, suggested I try to make it one more year. "If you go to work and you are not feeling well, just call me and let me know." She added, "If you don't feel better in a year, I'll help you with your paperwork and other benefits."

The support that I received from my community, the church, my clients, my family, the doctor, and my supervisor was awesome. I took my treatments. In a few months, I felt so much better and I continued working.

Once again I began to travel around within my state and to different states. I am still here and still working with the Diabetes CORE Group. At the time of this writing, it has been thirteen years since my diagnosis and surgery and I am still going strong. Thanks be to God.

I had planned on retiring in 2004. Yes, that was my plan. After I was diagnosed, however, I worked until I was 65 and continued working with the Diabetes CORE Group even after retirement from MUSC REACH 2010.

They gave me a certificate from the Cancer Center with "Congratulations" on it. I went through this with a positive mind while also telling others that there is nothing to it. I tell people to take care of themselves, follow doctor's orders, and most of all trust God. That is where I get my strength.

Since my diagnosis of breast cancer, I have recovered and planned even more community Diabetes CORE Group sessions; had more physical educational classes; appeared on more television shows; and also planned more cooking classes to help those in my community and beyond.

God has truly blessed my family. He has shined His light upon us. Thank God for that third Friday in August of 1973 and the miracles that followed. I am a stronger person because of them.

8

WHO IS FLORENE LINNEN?

As I was writing this book, I thought to myself, "Who am I to be writing anything? What are my credentials? Why should anyone listen to anything I have to say?" I mentioned this to someone and they suggested that I ask the community who they think I am. After all, they have been watching me over the years and working with me.

It had never occurred to me to ask what anyone thought about me. So, I asked the question and several people responded. I must say, I was very pleasantly, surprised at the responses.

While I travel a lot to different cities and communities, I cannot be everywhere. Hopefully, this book will reach areas I cannot reach, personally.

And as you read these letters, know that the person you are reading about is hoping that the information in this book will inspire you to go out and start something in your community. Most people will appreciate genuine help.

Who *is* Florene Linnen? Well, who do people say I am? You can read the responses for yourself in the letters that follow.

From: The Linnen Children

Who is Florene Linnen?

To us, her children, she is mama. She is intelligent and wise. Possessing less than an eighth grade education, she is equally at home speaking in front of community members, doctors or legislators.

She is greatly loved; the wife of a husband who supports her in everything that she initiates or participates in without a contrary word. A friend to many like-minded people who selflessly support her in whatever she undertakes.

She is influential, possessing a gift that enables her to mobilize healthcare professionals to volunteer their time for health fairs and health screenings. She is able to bring community members together to devote their time and efforts in order to make a difference in the lives of those diagnosed with diabetes through educational programs, and fitness classes. And when outside forces seek to exert control over the interests of our small community she is able to inform, and unify the community in opposition to such efforts.

She is selfless, often putting the needs and desires of others above her own, offering her time and resources, and sometimes our time and resources, to aid others who may be in need. From her volunteer work to help others sprang what would become the Diabetes CORE Group, a group dedicated to assisting underserved members of the community.

She is thankful and appreciative, constantly recognizing the efforts of those family members, friends, community members and healthcare professionals who support and enables the efforts she undertakes. And above all she thanks God for giving her the strength and ability to make a difference in the lives of others.

Perhaps more accurate than any description we might offer, she personifies the woman spoken of in Proverbs 31:10-31.

Who can find a virtuous woman? for her price is far above rubies.

The heart of her husband doth safely trust in her, so that he shall have no need of spoil.

She will do him good and not evil all the days of her life.

She seeketh wool, and flax, and worketh willingly with her hands.

She is like the merchants' ships; she bringeth her food from afar.

She riseth also while it is yet night, and giveth meat to her household, and a portion to her maidens.

She considereth a field, and buyeth it: with the fruit of her hands she planteth a vineyard.

She girdeth her loins with strength, and strengtheneth her arms.

She perceiveth that her merchandise is good: her candle goeth not out by night.

She layeth her hands to the spindle, and her hands hold the distaff.

She stretcheth out her hand to the poor; yea, she reacheth forth her hands to the needy.

She is not afraid of the snow for her household: for all her household are clothed with scarlet.

She maketh herself coverings of tapestry; her clothing is silk and purple.

Her husband is known in the gates, when he sitteth among the elders of the land.

She maketh fine linen, and selleth it; and delivereth girdles unto the merchant.

Strength and honour are her clothing; and she shall rejoice in time to come.

She openeth her mouth with wisdom; and in her tongue is the law of kindness.

She looketh well to the ways of her household, and eateth not the bread of idleness.

Her children arise up, and call her blessed; her husband also, and he praiseth her.

Many daughters have done virtuously, but thou excellest them all.

Favour is deceitful, and beauty is vain; but a woman that feareth the Lord, she shall be praised.

Give her of the fruit of her hands; and let her own works praise her in the gates.

This is Florene Linnen, she is wise, loved, influential, selfless, faithful and thankful to God. And while it is we, her children, who offer this tribute, it is the work that she has done that speaks more loudly than anything we might add.

Michael Anthony Linnen
Andrew James Linnen
Mark Lenard Linnen
Clarenda Michelle Linnen
Tranja Linnen
Herbert Lee Linnen, Jr.
Josh Anthony Linnen

From: Rosa Hurell

<u>To my sister Florene Linnen from your eldest sister Rosa Hurell</u>

My sister Florene is one of the most tenacious persons I know. From a child as we were growing up, she was firm in her ways and too determined to do what's right. Her outgoing personality has allowed her to encounter many people, she is a stranger to no one. When we were children, our mother and father raised us to be close and to take care of each other; to this day we have an unbreakable bond. Florene and I continue to support each other and has instilled in our children the importance of family. Being the eldest sister of 11 siblings, growing up in the south had its challenges. However, Florene and I faced those challenges with the upbringing of our parents to provide a productive and healthy way of life for our families.

Flo, you are a very special sister. I hold you near and dear to my heart. Growing up with you has made my life beautiful. You are filled with life and more importantly, the love of God in your heart. I have watched you grow up in a small southern town, and blossom into a beautiful and courageous mother, wife and a helper of the community. Flo, I've always admired your ability to speak your mind and your strength to take on tasks for the good of your family, community and church. The love I have for you goes without saying. When I think back on all the good times we've shared and sweet potato pies, my heart laughs. Flo, you are one in a million. The love and compassion you have for people is unchanging. I pray that God will continue to bless you and elevate you in all you endeavors. Once again, you are a beautiful and amazing sister. Love you, your oldest sister Rose.

Iron sharpeneth iron; so a man sharpeneth the countenance of his friend. Proverbs 27:17

From: Phyllys McKnight

What Florene Linnen means to me:

Growing up in a large southern family was a wonderful experience for me. Being the youngest sibling of 10 children gave me the opportunity to experience lots of parenting as well as teaching from different older family members.

I have known Florene all of my life and she was a very important part of my upbringing. She taught me the importance of hard work by her example. Back in the sixties and seventies she was working, as well as raising a family. Florene and her husband also had a tobacco farm that she helped with processing the product.

Florene also cared about her community and was always a community activist. Her goal was always trying to make it a better place to live.

Most importantly, her faith in God was always very evident and she lived a life style to reflect her belief. Overall, I would say that Florene was an important part of molding me into the successful, hardworking and caring adult that I am today.

Your sister Phyllys

Wishing you the best

From: Carolyn Jenkins, DrPH, APRN-BC-ADM, RD, CDE, FAAN

Florene Linnen, a champion, a leader, and my teacher and friend

Florene Linnen is a champion for her community, her state, and the nation! From my perspective, she has an MD, PhD, and EdD in life experiences and in motivating others to better manage their chronic health problems and take better care of their health. And although she openly shares that she does not have a high school degree, she certainly has the knowledge and experiences to facilitate community change. Why is her work so remarkable? She simply "makes things happen" rather than just talking about them.

She openly talks about her life experiences including that she has diabetes and is a breast cancer survivor. She continued to volunteer her time throughout her coping with her own health problems. She has often traveled in the middle of the night as a volunteer to help others. Her faith and her belief that people need a helping hand, and her positive attitude that "you can do it" motivates people to take positive actions. I personally know of several lives that have been saved because Florene Linnen, the tireless volunteer, went the extra mile and demonstrated that "we, the people" can make a difference. And she knows how to engage others to improve community life----for example, she had the Georgetown County Superintendent of Schools serving food and waiting tables for more than 150 persons who came together to raise money for medications for the uninsured and he seemed to enjoy it! Most weekends you can find her working with the Georgetown Diabetes CORE

Group (which she formed and continues to volunteer her time) to teach others about the importance of physical activity, eating healthy, and taking medications as prescribed to better manage their diabetes.

Ms Linnen has been a most instrumental partner in bringing more than $10 million in funding from the Centers for Disease Control and Prevention to improve disparities for African Americans with diabetes in Charleston and Georgetown Counties. Most importantly, she has translated the science of diabetes to the entire county of Georgetown and has worked tirelessly with multiple groups all over the state. She actively works with all ages but focuses on youth and older adults to improve diabetes outcomes. She has worked with the Medical University of South Carolina College of Nursing and the Diabetes Initiative of South Carolina as both an employee and a volunteer since 1999. Diabetes-related amputations in African American men have decreased by about 50% and much of this has been because of her hard work and efforts to make a difference.

Additionally, it was because of her leadership that the MUSC REACH 2010: Charleston and Georgetown Diabetes Coalition received the very prestigious National Community-Campus Partnership for Health Award in May 2006. Her contributions can be seen on the documentary at: **http://depts.washington.edu/ccph/awards2006-reach2010.html**

She has accompanied me to many national meetings related to health and her talks are always so relevant for the audiences. People (from US Secretary of Health to other volunteers and health professionals) line up to shake her hand and congratulate her on the difference she is making in the lives of others. Congressman Clyburn and Senator Graham have both recognized her efforts in speeches on health disparities.

I know of no one person who has volunteered more of their time to make a significant difference in their community and state of South Carolina than Florene Linnen. Most of us receive monetary rewards. While she simply works to "improve life in her community" through teaching others, through working endlessly to convert an abandoned school into the Choppee Health Complex, maintaining a healthy water supply for her community, and helping Georgetown to be selected as an "All American County." She fights the war on poverty and disease, and creates a world with equal treatment for all. I am proud to call her my teacher and my friend.

Carolyn Jenkins, DrPH, APRN-BC-ADM, RD, CDE, FAAN
Professor and Ann Darlington Edwards Endowed Chair
Co-Director for Community Engagement
South Carolina Translational Research Institute
College of Nursing Room 408
Medical University of South Carolina
99 Jonathan Lucas, Box 250160
Charleston, South Carolina 29425
Phone: (843) 792-4625
Cell: (843) 697-9089

From: Morant & Morant, Attorneys at Law, 1022 Prince St., Georgetown, S.C.

It recently came to my attention that a book is going to be written about the life of Florene Linnen. My friends and I have always wondered how Florene could remain so loyal and dedicated to a cause that benefitted so many. Educating her community and others about diabetes is what Florene will always be known for.

I have known Florene for more than twenty years. She is one of a kind. Her uplifting spirit, dedication and commitment to assist others are as strong today as they were twenty years ago. Her common sense approach to the many challenges in our communities today is admirable.

Florene has the uncanny ability to work with others from all walks of life. From her humble beginning, Florene has far exceeded the expectations that many had of her.

It is really great that the life and legacy of my dear friend will now be shared with so many who are not aware of her background and the personal struggles she has endured while working to enhance the livelihood of others.

I can only hope that the full life story of Florene Linnen is captured in what proposes to be a great reading for the curious minds.

Always wishing you the best Florene.

Johnny Morant

From: Isaac L. Pyatt, Sr.

Mrs. Florene Linnen is a luminary to her community and to Georgetown County as a whole. I first met Mrs. Linnen some twenty-five plus years ago. And at that time she was very involved with the Waccamaw Economic opportunity Council, Inc. where she was as a harbinger for the underprivileged in rural areas of Georgetown County.

Mrs. Florene and I have been a part of many of the same organizations and committees where I witnessed her as a pacesetter-giving her best effort in every situation. She consistently shows a willingness to go above and beyond for people and has the natural ability to get things done.

Most importantly, Mrs. Linnen is a person of solid character. She has a heart for serving the Lord, and she is a woman of great integrity and high moral standards. Mrs. Linnen has demonstrated an outstanding ability to work within a wide variety of circumstances with poise and class. She unfailingly treats others with both kindness and respect, and models Christ-like leadership very effectively.

Mrs. Florene's eminence with the Georgetown County Diabetes Community Outreach Resources & Education (CORE) initiative has made her popular across the state of South Carolina. She has worked tirelessly to educate, empower and advocate for changes in the health system for people with diabetes in the Georgetown community.

Congratulations Mrs. Linnen. Your longstanding commitment to Georgetown County and your community make us all proud to know you!

Isaac L. Pyatt, Sr., Chief Magistrate, Georgetown County Summary Court

**From: Virginia Thomas,
P.O. Box 20342, Charleston, S.C.**

I met Mrs. Florene on the first day of the first meeting of the community and MUSC partners. During the session we all introduced ourselves. After the meeting ended she walked up to me saying "Hi, I'm Florene Linnen and you are Virginia Thomas. I was told I need to meet you." And the rest is history. It was the beginning of a collaboration and friendship that has lasted over 16 years. She has been and is an inspiration to me and serves as a role model as well.

Florene is a strong community advocate with a foundation built upon a caring attitude, a love for people and a drive to make things happen for the communities she serves. She has been the driving force of the CORE Group since its beginning. Does she say no? Not often. Does she try to do all she can? Yes, always. She was not afraid to take the trainings offered and made great use of all the education she got saying: "If you show me. I may not learn as fast as everyone else but when I get it, I've got it." She learned quickly and never stopped learning or sharing what she knew. Her enthusiasm seems to be boundless.

As a community worker, she helped all she came in contact with get educated, connect to and obtain available resources. She worked hard to make information known to rural Georgetown and surrounding communities. Her efforts improved the area opportunities and brought notice to many communities. Mrs. Flo became a household name.

As a community health worker for MUSC she ran an organization collaboration that worked to connect everyone they met anywhere they met with the rest of the world facing diabetes and its complications. She has worn so many hats it is not hard to consider her a super-advocate. We traveled to many conferences and meetings where she inspired listeners to return to their communities and keep trying to help all they contact.

So let me tell you about Flo: Mrs. Linnen spearheaded the necessary support to establish the Choppee Regional Primary Health located in the rural area of Georgetown. This complex includes a medical center, aerobics exercise classrooms, a clinic for regular and especially diabetes patients and prevention office, Waccamaw Mental Health Center, Georgetown County Drug and Alcohol Center, Georgetown County Youth Prevention, the CORE Coalition, after school tutorial program and park and recreation services.

Mrs. Linnen has coordinated and inspired numerous activities to include:

Director of the Georgetown District African Methodist Episcopal Churches Health Ministry's in Churches

Daily walking groups in three different communities in the rural areas

Annual Diabetes University Health Day/Fair which includes lectures and numerous screenings for sugar diabetes, cholesterol, foot checks, body fat, etc. This function included over 300 participants

Diabetes social program for diabetes patients and their spouses

Diabetes Banquet-a fundraiser that attracts over 250 participants

Monthly lectures and health tips on a local radio station, WLMC Georgetown;

Work with the Medical University of South Carolina, REACH 2010 Program. This program allowed her to conduct workshops on an as needed basis, visit the homes of diabetes patients, and set up group educational lectures in the different community centers and churches;

And she organized a campaign for youth diabetes awareness workshops;

For over ten years, Mrs. Linnen participated on the panel for South Carolina Rural Communities, a Health Disparity Educational Program airing on Channel 7 Educational Television, and assisted the Center for Disease Control (CDC) at the Washington State CDC Office and the Boston, Massachusetts Office with information on the effects of diabetes in the rural communities.

So that's a little something about Flo, my mentor and friend and the best community advocate in the Low Country.

Sincerely

Virginia Thomas

From: Carrie Butler

I was given the opportunity and privilege to meet Mrs. Florene Linnen, my cousin, when I was just a little girl. I remember this beautiful, smart, and charismatic young lady. I knew some 50 years ago that she would make a difference in this world. As the founder of the Georgetown Diabetes CORE Group and advocate for individual empowerment through community-level health initiatives, Mrs. Linnen has had a big impact on my life. I attended several community outreach workshops on diabetes education sponsored by Mrs. Linnen. I am someone who is living with diabetes. Through Mrs. Linnen's dedication and hard work to educate our community on this disease, I learned that I did not have to resign myself to the complications and impacts of diabetes. Mrs. Linnen taught me that through the power of knowledge, I can be in control of this disease.

Carrie Butler

From: Rev. Joe Canteen

Who is Florene Linnen?

Florene is a pioneer who is willing to take a stand, willing to fight for others who won't fight for themselves, and willing to walk the extra mile. She is a Godly woman. She is a community activist who believes that everybody is somebody in God's eye sight. Florene is a loving mother with a family who respects her for what she stands for in the community, at the state level, and on the national level. No distance was too far to travel when it came time for her to be a blessing to someone. Florene is a giving person who knows that it is better to give than to receive. She is a friend you can count on who has a cool head and a warm heart. God is definitely first in her life. Florene has served on many boards in the church. She is always willing to give of herself to help in whatever ways she can.

May God keep on blessing you over and over again.

Blessings,

Rev. Joe Canteen

(Peachy)

From: Arthur Ford

Who is Florene Linnen?

Florene Linnen is first a Christian. She loves God and lover her neighbor. Her relationship with Christ is the foundation of everything that she attempts.

Florene is a wife, mother, grandmother, aunt, cousin, sister, and friend. Family is very important to her and this is made evident in the way her family responds to her and how this witness of fame, joy, and love is spread in the community. Florene is a community activist. She takes great pride in standing up for members of her community. She is present at school activities, school board meetings and county council functions. Florene makes her presence known at every election. She understands that it is important to be concerned but more importantly to act.

Florene is a health crusader. She is very concerned about the health of all citizens. She has established the Diabetes Core Group. Florene continues to work on these issues. She is concerned about the health disparities among the poor African American community. She brings timely information to the community to remedy the problem.

Florene is a renaissance woman. A woman for all seasons; she is comfortable among the rich and famous and yet she maintains the common touch.

Arthur

From: Abie Ladson

A Letter of Congratulations

Florene is a natural born leader. Her greatest strength is to help people. She does her best in a challenging and organized environment. She is a good talker and listener. She is task oriented and one who gets results.

She has made her church a better place to worship. Her interest in health has made it possible for her community to have safe drinking water and a sewer system.

She is also an internal optimist. She never stops dreaming of ways in which to make things better. Her role in organizing the Georgetown Diabetes Core Group is a good example of her optimistic personality. The impact of this organization can be felt throughout the medical community in Georgetown County and the state of South Carolina.

She is at her best when helping others.

Abie Ladson

May 5, 2015

From: Missionary Evelyn F. Lance

To My Dearest Friend,

Florene, I am writing these words of praise and love to you, a great woman of God who realizes her long anticipation and dream of writing a book to further encourage and enlighten people on how to take care of their health issues such as diabetes, stroke, heart, and kidney diseases. You have done a marvelous job in these areas, plus more.

You have helped many, many people throughout the surrounding communities and other places. Your hard work ethics and diligence helped me to attend many workshops learning to care for my diabetes. Today, my diabetes is under very good control. Thanks to you and all of the information you made possible for me and others.

I must say, "to God Be the Glory." There were many days that we went to Charleston and Columbia to learn about some of the disparities in our bodies. These places you would agree to visit.

You went the extra mile in order to learn something new to help us who needed to be able to take better take care of ourselves. Again, I say "To God Be the Glory" because you were not always sure of where to go but you always trusted God, and He always had someone right where you needed them to direct you. You even had a policeman to escort you to your destination. Those were some good days. (Smile)

Trust in the Lord with all your heart and lean not unto thine own understanding.

In all thy ways acknowledge him, and he will direct thy paths. (Proverbs 3, vs.5-6)

Congratulations and best wishes.

Your friend and sister in the Lord.

Missionary Evelyn F. Lance

August 26, 2015

From: Keith Moore

"Many are called, few are chosen."

When I look at the many works that Mrs. Florene Linnen has done and continues to do in our community, it is clear to see she had to have been chosen and anointed by God.

Hello, my name is Keith Moore, manager of Brown's Ferry Water Company. I would like to take this time to applaud Mrs. Linnen for her servitude and commitment to the Brown's Ferry community.

Most people would probable associate Mrs. Flo with the great works she has done with the Diabetes CORE. This is only one of many local causes that she is involved in. It would take quite some time to tell it all. I'll share how I came to know Mrs. Flo.

My first encounter happened at a time when there had been a few issues with our water company. Members of the community had gathered for a meeting at Brown's Ferry Elementary School to discuss ways to solve the problem. After hours of serious discussions, it was decided to elect Mrs. Linnen as the chairperson to look into the matters pertaining to the water company. I remember sitting there thinking to myself, "out of all these strong men that are present, the community turned to Mrs. Linnen for this task." I thought to myself that the men should have been ashamed of themselves, turning to a woman. But I thank God that I had the opportunity to get to know Mrs. Flo. I realized what those men knew that I didn't. They knew that in spite of it being a man or woman, many are called, but Mrs. Flo was chosen.

Congratulations,

Keith

From: Murray Vernon

July 15, 2015

To Whom It May Concern

This letter is on behalf of Mrs. Florene Linnen. I met Florene many years ago at Nazareth AME Church where both of us are members and very active in the Church Christian Journey and Development.

Florene is very much involved in the Church Health Ministry as well as Georgetown County and South Carolina. She is the founder of the Georgetown County Diabetes CORE Group that have had a major impact on the education of the prevention and treatment for diabetes.

Mrs. Linnen is recognized throughout South Carolina for her work in the field of Health Care in Georgetown County.

Murray Vernon

FLORENE LINNEN

PART II

THE

GEORGETOWN

COUNTY DIABETES

C.O.R.E. GROUP

9

DEFINING THE DIABETES CORE GROUP

The Life Changing Invitation

In June of 1997, I was invited to a diabetes workshop – *Diabetes Today* - which was sponsored by the South Carolina Department of Health and Environmental Control (DHEC). The class was intended to funnel information out into the surrounding communities. The attendees were encouraged to share the information they received at the class with their families and friends as well as other people in their communities.

Well, I traveled to Myrtle Beach for two days - June 26th and 27th. I learned more in those 2 days than I had learned in the entire time that I was a diabetic. And I had been a diabetic for 16 years. At the time of the class on June 26th and 27th, I was 54 years old.

The speakers for the event were very informative. This was information that I immediately knew I would be taking back home to help my community, family and friends.

Very soon afterwards, I started giving presentations at my church. Then, I decided to do a survey of the people in my community and nearby communities including, but not limited to, Dunbar, Choppee, Oatland, and Pee Dee. These are all very rural areas.

Having worked at Waccamaw EOC for many years, I had picked up the skills to create forms. So, I created a form to assess the health status of the people in our neighboring communities. I spoke to people in the churches, in the streets, and anywhere I found them. Wanting to do a good job, I asked for the help of the people I already knew and people I was just meeting to help administer the survey and find out how people were really doing.

As a result of the survey, we found out that there were over 75 people that were either diabetic or were at risk for diabetes in the communities. People were losing their limbs as well as having problems with their eyes. One community member said to me that she lost her vision because of diabetes. It was clear that we had a very serious problem that had been left unnoticed.

After seeing the survey results, I solicited the help of several people to come together concerning working on diabetes education along with me. Many promised, but when the meeting was actually held, only two people showed up. Needless to say, I was very disappointed.

Never the less, I kept on working, developing my ideas and doing presentations whenever the opportunity presented itself. Those two people that showed up at that initial meeting worked with me until we got more people on board. Lena Meyers, Mary Greggs and I were a committee of 3. The committee began to brainstorm about other things that could be done to move things forward.

Not knowing what else to do, I began praying and thinking, "What must I do to help my community?"

One Sunday morning, as I got out of bed and started making the bed, the Spirit brought that diabetes workshop that I attended in Myrtle Beach, back to my mind. I said, "But Lord, I have no money. What do I do?" An internal voice said to me, "Get support from the community. Ask and it shall be done."

At that very moment I began to plan a little farther. You see, I knew without a doubt that it was going to work by the help of the Lord.

The next step: I scheduled a community meeting at Dickerson AME Church in the city of Georgetown, South Carolina. This meeting was focused on the entire county and it was held on September 15, 1997. On that day, I did not even think about the fact that I only had a 6th grade education. Driven by faith and love, I had written a speech and I used it to address people from all over Georgetown County. We had a total of about 80 people from the different communities present at this meeting.

My desire was to make sure that everyone who needed help got help. And I was always enlisting the support of anyone who was willing to give help. There was no money to pay anyone. It was all done by good will.

Disregarding any perceived shortcomings in my life, I gave a heartfelt speech which captivated the listeners. The meeting was a success.

From that meeting, I was able to reach out to even more people in additional communities. This event was the beginning of what was to become known as The

Georgetown County Diabetes CORE Group - an organization which would come to impact thousands of lives across the United States and abroad.

Diabetes is a very serious disease, but with proper care, you can control it.

Speech from the 1st County Wide Meeting

Thank you all for coming. It is certainly a pleasure to see each and every one of you today. The purpose that we are gathered here tonight is to discuss the seriousness of diabetes.

Some people may say that a telephone conversation is not important, but I say to you that the content of the conversation is the important thing.

One important call that I made was to Project IDEAS and spoke with Miss Tressia Delvin. This conversation made a great impact on my life. Miss Nesmith invited me to attend a diabetes training session that was being held that very day.

I accepted the invitation and it was certainly a blessing from the Lord, it was a prayer being answered. I was searching for answers and more information about this condition called diabetes.

I have been a diabetic for a number of years and have learned more in just two sessions with this group than I have in the past. The information that I received gave me a new outlook on life and a greater determination to press onward.

I went back to my church and immediately began to spread the news of the things that I learned. I wanted to share with those who have encountered this illness and to tell others what to do to try and prevent it.

This is one illness that sometimes people take for granted. It is a serious illness in that it can cause you to lose the use of vital organs such as your kidneys, your eyesight and the loss of your limbs.

You lose your limbs in that the least scratch, cut, scrape or nick can become infected. If the infected area is not treated properly and immediately, it can lead to amputation.

Diabetes can also lead to heart conditions and even fatal heart attacks. But learning how to eat, what to eat, and ways to prepare your food along with proper rest and exercise is the best recipe for a long and healthy life.

We need Community CORE persons that will take vital information back to their various communities. I will be the Resource and Information person to distribute information to these people. The American Diabetes Association, Project IDEAS, and Miss Cindy Epps, Health Coordinator of Georgetown Memorial hospital, along with others will provide information to be distributed.

Another goal of this CORE group will be to focus on prevention care for our youth and to give support and present vital information to family members of a diabetic. If your diet is a problem we will have a nutritionist come and guide you through the preparation of healthy meals. They will show you how to make your meals tasty without using all the things like ham hocks and fat back. You will be shown how to substitute various meat, cheeses, and even spices.

We are on a serious mission and that mission is to take the best care of this body that God has given us. Whether you are a diabetic or not, you and you alone are responsible for your health. We will be a support group, give out vital information, offer advice and assistance, but you are responsible for the final results.

The Purpose

Within six months after the meeting at Dickerson AME Church, *The Georgetown County Diabetes Community Outreach Resource & Education Group* (Diabetes CORE Group) was formed. The purpose of the Diabetes CORE Group was to *educate, advocate, empower, and make people aware of diabetes and its health related issues.*

The meeting at Dickerson AME Church was successful in expanding our outreach efforts. We were able to reach more people and we had more volunteers come forth.

I told the committee and the various people who were donating their time that we should have a banquet and name it *Health Resource Banquet.* Everyone liked that idea. So, we began delegating duties to each person on the committee, and also the other people who volunteered.

This became our first event and it was a big step in carrying out our purpose. It was not a fundraiser, however. We only wanted to improve awareness. The event was held in March, 1998.

For the event, we contacted health care providers. Between 20 and 30 of the health care providers, to whom we reached out, answered our calls. They were very generous and eager to help. Their role was to provide information for the community according to their various specialties. They would do presentations at the banquet and set up health displays.

The next part of our plan was to figure out how to get the money to purchase the food for the banquet. Once again, the Spirit spoke to my heart: "Go to Mr. Joe." (He gave $100.00.); "Go to Brother Pea." (He gave $50.00.) By the time I went around and called and pleaded to all of the people who came to mind, I had $1,000.00 to purchase food for the banquet. Then I said to myself, "Look at Jesus. He promised to provide." The banquet was free for attendees.

The purpose of this event was to assist people who had this abnormal disease - diabetes - and help create a healthier group of people and healthier communities.

When the day came for the banquet, I couldn't believe that we had over 100 people at that banquet. Many people have asked me why the event was so successful. I tell them that I have worked in the community all of my life. People have always known me to be honest and truthful, and they knew that I just wanted to help my community to be a healthier community. That was the key to our success in getting the communities involved. I am grateful for the people who extended themselves to help with this project.

One day, a young lady invited me to her church to do a presentation. I did the presentation willingly with no hesitation because I was on a mission and I was a person who loved to talk. It didn't matter when I was asked to do a presentation. I was always ready to go.

After the presentation, the young lady said to me, "Mrs. Flo, if I had this information years ago, my granddaddy might still be alive and he would not have lost his legs." The young lady's name was Joyce. Joyce decided to join the Diabetes CORE Group because she also wanted to help educate people about diabetes.

I remember sitting in my office one day when Joyce came in and said to me, "I have something I want to tell you." I gave her my full attention. I wondered what this was about. She continued, "I know this is your baby, but we have been dating for a while." I was really happy to hear this because she had knowledge that could really help me with my work. And this meant she would be staying for a while. After some time, my son came to me and said, "I bought her a ring." Well, I just knew he had told her. But guess what? I was the one who told her. I spoiled the surprise. Anyway, she said "yes" and that young lady is now my daughter-in-law. She has been an enormous help with carrying out the purpose of the Diabetes CORE Group.

The Power of People

After our first event, the *Health Resource Banquet*, we began to distribute flyers about what the Diabetes CORE Group was doing. I was still working at Waccamaw EOC. We recruited some volunteers from among the people I met through my job at Waccamaw EOC to help me with my campaign against diabetes. I was able to set up a plan and work the plan.

We found that we needed even more volunteers to pass out the flyers. As a field worker for Waccamaw EOC, I knew many young children in the communities who had bicycles. They could use their bicycles to cover a lot of ground and pass out more flyers. I asked for their help and those children were ready to go. I have always had a good relationship with the children and the adults in the communities and wherever I found myself. Again, God's grace.

The health care providers in Georgetown County were very charitable to the communities in providing information. The community in which I live is very rural. People didn't like coming into our community because we didn't have street lights. It is very dark at night. We have long, dark and sometimes curvy roads. It is the same for the neighboring communities. Education about diabetes and high blood pressure was not present because no one wanted to come out into the country.

Well, I went where no one wanted to go. There was one young lady from the Georgetown Hospital System who traveled all over the northwestern side of Georgetown County with me. The two of us drove around together and went into people's homes, to centers, and churches to demonstrate to them how to cook and eat healthy. To give you an idea of the significance of our efforts, let me point out that the northwest side of Georgetown County consists of about 7,000 people, over an area of about 35 very rural miles.

I am so thankful for the help of the communities. Traveling over the highways over these long country roads with my kind of work has been tiring and difficult. Sometimes I couldn't find the directions to my destination, but I always had someone with me to help. I remember one night when I had an interview with a television channel in Columbia, South Carolina and we did not get home until 3 o'clock the next morning. Six of us were in the car and we were as lost as a bat. Never the less, those sisters were happy and didn't get upset. They counted it all joy because they supported me and the Diabetes CORE Group. When people work together, it makes life's challenges a whole lot easier to handle.

Funding

Sitting home one night in 1999, a friend of mine called and said, "Mrs. Flo, if you could get me 125 letters, you might be eligible to get some funds for diabetes. Someone said that there was a storm going on in Georgetown with a Florene Linnen and diabetes. Check her out." This was the same woman who I had called, when I got invited to that class in June of 1997. Well, we went to the communities and the churches and we got enough letters. The letters explained how badly we needed education on diabetes in Georgetown County.

After those letters, doors began to open. The Racial and Ethnic Approaches to Community Health (REACH) 2010, Dr. Carolyn Jenkins and The Medical University of South Carolina joined forces with me. Dr. Jenkins and The Medical University of South Carolina had just started the REACH 2010 program. That program was designed to educate people about diabetes. Dr. Jenkins was the director of the project. She came to Georgetown and met with me. After our discussion, she offered me a job with MUSC REACH 2010. Since I was still a few years from retirement, I told her that I would work part-time with their agency. I was already working a full-time job.

I began to travel to Charleston for more training and began meeting new people in the MUSC REACH 2010 program. We agreed that I would work for MUSC REACH 2010 for 3 hours per day on activities for the Diabetes CORE Group. Being a part of the MUSC REACH 2010 program provided funding to help educate the people in Georgetown County about diabetes, including the previously overlooked rural areas. My heart was glad.

After a while, Joyce, my daughter-in-law, who had been working with me, decided to get a job because the Diabetes CORE Group is an organization staffed by volunteers, and she needed to earn an income. I was left alone in the office.

Without a lot of technical skills, I was doubtful about continuing with the work. So, I said to my husband, "I think I am going to give it up." This was the year 2008, the year that I retired from MUSC REACH 2010.

I was unable to do a fundraiser that year. We did not have money to assist clients. The more I thought about it, the worse I felt. I said to myself, "the Diabetes CORE Group is your life and you will never be satisfied. I am going to stand and stand strong for the people." A week later a man came into my office and said, "Mrs. Linnen, you said you are having an upcoming *Healthy Day* and I want to help." A few weeks later, a lady came into the office and wanted to help.

The Diabetes CORE Group was still alive. God is mighty and He is good and He will provide our needs. Remember, when things begin to look so dark, God steps in. My heart is to see people happy. I often think about my father saying to me, "Be happy and owe no man anything other than to love them."

The MUSC REACH 2010 program ended in 2010. The Diabetes CORE Group, however, continues its mission of educating people on the subject of diabetes. Dr. Carolyn Jenkins continues working with the Diabetes CORE Group by helping with funding from time to time.

The Diabetes CORE Group continues to have fundraising events to support our efforts. Our organization is a labor of love and it is run entirely on donations and the help of volunteers.

We Have a Home

I have traveled to different places and I have done many workshops in South Carolina on the subject of diabetes, diabetes symptoms and related illnesses. Our work with diabetes was very successful in helping the people in the communities. After a few years of the Diabetes CORE Group being in existence, someone came to me and said, "You are doing a great job with diabetes. You need to get an office." I had been working out of my home all of this time. So, this sounded like a good idea to me.

Well, right away, I made some phone calls and asked for help from the communities. We called a meeting to discuss the subject of getting a doctor's office. The meeting was held at Mt. Sinai Baptist Church on Brown's Ferry Road across from Brown's Ferry Elementary School. The church was packed with eager participants to learn about diabetes and the work we were doing. A committee was formed which was called, "the Steering Committee for the Doctor's Office." Fourteen community members were elected to work with me on this committee.

They selected me to go and talk to the higher powers - the County Administrator and South Carolina Primary Health Care Association. They told me that only two (2) people in the community wanted a doctor's office.

They did say, however, that if I could show them that more than 2 people wanted a doctor's office, they would definitely work with me on getting that doctor's office in the community.

So, the committee set up a community meeting in Georgetown (the city). People came from all over Georgetown County from all of the rural areas. The building was packed and overflowing. People were standing all on the outside. At the conclusion of this meeting, we had proof that more than 2 people wanted a doctor's office in the rural part of Georgetown County.

Meetings were held to discuss the renovation of the old school - Choppee High School - to contain the doctor's office. Community members came together to clean the building and set up the offices. We called a meeting of all community leaders and health agencies for the purpose of determining the new name of the building. MUSC REACH 2010 members were at all community meetings, as well.

The building was named the *Choppee Health Complex* - a one-stop shop. The Diabetes CORE Group's office was right there with the doctor's office.

Seven years after I attended the workshop that started a health revolution in Georgetown, South Carolina, we had a home for the organization that had evolved from that workshop. The Georgetown County Diabetes CORE Group, now, had a home. The year was 2004. The official opening date would be in 2005.

The work began. Now that we had a home, we were going to set up a one-stop shop. The Diabetes CORE Group, the Center for Mental Health, DHEC, St. James Santee Center all were going to be staffed with a director at the one-stop shop, which would be located in the old Choppee High School building.

The community was overjoyed about this because the school that they attended was the same place they would be going to receive health care. The school which had started holding classes in 1959 had been closed and the structure was left standing. What a blessing that turned out to be.

Many people of the north western communities have worked long and hard here at the one-stop shop center. The Diabetes CORE Group uses this location for diabetes education, exercise classes, and cooking classes. We have, also, planted a garden to encourage people to eat right. Someone from the community donated a parcel of land to serve as the community garden. The property is near the center. So it is easy to get to and maintain. I enlist the help of the youth of the community to pack the vegetables for patients with diseases such as cancer and diabetes and related illnesses.

At the one-stop shop, we have various agencies to assist the clients with their needs. We have a home from which to administer care for the residents of the North Western side of Georgetown County. This is history for us – help *outside* of the city.

Our one-stop shop is the same building where we went to school in our youth. The name is slightly changed and we now go there for our health needs. Having this center also reduced travel time for patients who needed care.

After many workshops, speaking engagements, and television appearances on the subject of diabetes and related diseases, at the age of 61, I was getting ready to retire. My goal was to pay off my bills and buy myself a new car. But instead, in 2004, I defeated cancer and the Diabetes CORE Group found a home. Today, I am retired, but I am still working from that home – The Choppee Health Complex - as a volunteer.

My husband said to me once, "I do believe you will give your head off your body, if you think you could live without it." My husband, bless his heart, supports me with everything that I do in the community. We have been married for 55 years and we can still live together peacefully.

10

DIABETES CORE GROUP ACTIVITIES

Diabetes is serious, but you can live with it. Control and watch what you eat, and exercise often. That is my song and I sing it everywhere I go. It has been almost 20 years since I began my mission to share information about diabetes and help save lives and limbs. We continue to teach classes related to diabetes, and cooking, and eating healthy. We also educate people in their homes.

I love going into the homes of the clients. I never went to a home and got turned away. Sometimes they are slow to accept me, but when I engage them in the conversation about the seriousness of diabetes and the prospect of prolonging their lives, they open up. They begin to talk about themselves and other family members and how diabetes has affected them.

The Diabetes CORE Group is a community initiative. Helping and caring about people with diabetes is a service we provide to the Georgetown communities. We also work to bring about changes in the health system.

The Diabetes CORE Group had a very humble beginning. It was born out of love for people and a simple desire to make a difference. I never could have imagined how far it would reach. In stepping back and taking a look at the impact of a single notion, "to share information," I realize that this is something that could be done by anyone. It's not complicated at all.

Anyone can share information and ask others to help. With commitment and love, people can make a difference anywhere. And it is my hope that writing this book will inspire someone to do just that. It doesn't take a PhD. In my case, it didn't even take a high school diploma.

That being said, I am not encouraging anyone to drop out of school. Quite the contrary. I admonish you to get as much education as possible. You can never know too much. And by all means, even if you are not in school, become an avid reader. Knowledge is priceless. Where ever you are in you educational journey, even if you are a drop out, it doesn't mean that you cannot make a difference.

It starts with an idea and continues with one step at a time, and asking others to help. When you love people and you love what you are doing, ways can be made. And people will help you. Not everyone, of course. But you cannot let the naysayers keep you from making your contribution to your community.

In this section of the book, I share with you some activities that were done to help change the lives of people living with diabetes in Georgetown, South Carolina. As we progressed, we attracted the attention of people in other areas of the state and the country.

These are simple steps that can be done by anyone. Or, possibly, they can be adapted for your area or your cause. So whether it is diabetes or some other health condition of which you want to cause change, I hope that you will be able to use some of these ideas to start something in your community.

Affiliates/Partnerships

As I have mentioned before, the Diabetes CORE Group is an organized, volunteer effort funded by donations. During the life of the Diabetes CORE Group, we have developed relationships with several organizations. These relationships allow us to greatly expand the services that we are able to offer to the communities.

The Diabetes CORE Group sponsors educational efforts regarding prevention, early detection and treatment of diabetes, which we could not do alone. We are grateful for the support, partnership and sponsorship of our affiliates:

- REACH U.S. SEA-CEED of Charleston, S.C.
- MUSC College of Nursing of Charleston, S.C.
- DHEC of Georgetown, S.C.
- DIABETES INITIATIVE of South Carolina
- Georgetown Parks & Recreation
- St. James Santee Health Center

Training for Diabetics

In 1997, I started out by talking to people, asking questions, and sharing information about diabetes. I wanted people to live and keep their limbs, if possible. So, I asked people to help. And little by little, people joined in. We were able to help more and more people by having different community events with the focus on diabetes awareness.

People want to help people, who want to help people. That modest beginning has grown and resulted in many classes designed to help people live longer, healthier lives with diabetes. The Diabetes CORE Group went into the different communities and set up classes and support groups.

People were very receptive and took advantage of the help provided. One client said that her A1C went down so low that her doctor said, "You must have been to Florene Linnen's diabetes class."

These are simple classes and they would be great for any community. People are more likely to take advantage of help when the help they need is in their own community. We have listed here some classes for your consideration.

Diabetes Education

We offer workshops and training programs such as :
   a) *Choose to Live* (Teaching how to choose the right food, when to go to the doctor, etc.),
   b) *Diabetes 101* (Teaching about diabetes and related diseases),
   c) *Power to Prevent* (Teaching prevention).

Classes are taught in the center and out in the communities.

Computer Health Classes

We encouraged people to learn how to use modern technology, and how to access and find reliable health information online. People volunteered to teach us how to use the computer. They taught us how to look for information out of the National Networks of Libraries of Medicine in Bethesda, MD. The students being taught computer skills and the art of looking up medical information included seniors. Some of the students were clients; some were Diabetes CORE Group volunteers. Currently, this class is on demand. The original classes included 30-35 people; about 10-12 of them wanted to know more about the computer. During this initial program, MUSC REACH 2010 gave me a laptop to use. I was happy to learn how to use the computer.

Healthy Cooking Classes

The Diabetes CORE Group teaches cooking classes to promote healthy eating for people with diabetes. As a part of these cooking classes, we also teach about the types of food that are good for diabetics and the types of food that are not. We also give out pamphlets to help support the information presented in the classes.

Initially, the Diabetes CORE Group sent out letters to the health directors at the churches and had classes at the churches. Classes were also held at community centers. We drove around, sometimes, and set up wherever people would let us, and demonstrated proper cooking of food.

Today, we hire professional cooks to teach our classes. But in the beginning, we did not have the funding to do this. My youngest son, Herbie, is a cook and he knew food very well. He helped out tremendously. The people did not know how to cook the food properly or which foods were best. My son and I held the classes together. Herbie cooked the foods and did the cooking training; I talked to the people about food.

Fitness and Wellness Class

Exercise classes were offered once a week at the center. The equipment was donated. At the time of this writing, we have temporarily had to discontinue the classes at the center due to space issues. We also organized walking groups in the different communities.

One evening I started thinking, "What can I do to make things more inviting to the community?" Boom! "Why not do a *Zumba* class?" We did and that was a success. We had a great time. Senior citizens and young adults came out for the class. We had to hire someone to come in and teach the class.

Another class that was very successful was *line dancing*. People love to have fun. So we try to have fun activities so that people will not think of it as work, but as something exciting.

Classes on *smoking* were taught and showed how cigarettes turn your lungs a different color. This was an on-going class. We had a company come in with their equipment to show what happens to the lungs. St. James Santee Health Center taught me how to use the equipment so that I could conduct the class. Classes were either held in the center or out in the community.

Our physical fitness class had a meeting once a week at the center. We discussed health issues and walking. The attendees were given pedometers. They wore it during the week and brought it to the next meeting where we discussed the results, how to walk, and how much time they walked.

When I began in 1997, every morning at 5 o'clock I walked. Walking is a very good and easy exercise.

Nutrition Education Programs

Knowing your sugar number was one lesson I taught the residents of Georgetown County and anyone who would listen. Pay attention to your A1C, lipids, blood pressure, and microallbumin and get an eye exam. If you know your A1C is high for the last three months, then you must exercise, eat more fruits and vegetables, and stop drinking sodas in order to get your A1C at 7 or below. With diabetes, you can't control your health if you don't know your numbers or what to look for or what questions to ask the doctor.

One day I decided to try a new strategy. I said to myself, "Why don't you think about a family who eats everything?" They eat everything and don't realize that it is harmful to their health, especially if they are a diabetic.

So, I began to think about a title for this project. The thought came to me, "Call it *CORE Family.*" The process would be to talk to one family at a time about coming into their home and going through their kitchen cabinets. We would take the bad food out and replace it with healthy food and fresh vegetables from the community garden.

This program would be presented to the clients as, "Welcome to the new you and life and most importantly to a new family."

So, Information was given to different families with ongoing resourceful information, access to a pharmacist, medicine, access to nutrition and one on one consultation sessions.

We received a grant to purchase food for the program. The families were taken out shopping and taught how to read food labels. Healthy eating and healthy cooking lessons were taught.

We went into the homes and checked the kitchen cabinets and took out the food that was not healthy, or had too much salt. We, then, purchased food with low sodium or no salt. That in conjunction with healthier foods and fresh vegetables resulted in the families losing weight.

Entire families participated and were amazed at the results. The families talked about their results, how their lives changed, eating habits, what was discontinued, complete behavioral and life change.

We taught the communities about a complete life style change. Six (6) families participated over a period of 3 months. Two other Diabetes CORE Group members and I conducted the program.

We finished the *CORE Family* program and then this came to my mind - A Fashion Show. Now that they have lost weight, let's show off their new sizes and new outfits.

The men and women dressed up and we had a fashion show and dinner. Community members donated services to do the hair and nails of the participants. The blessing was that they were happy and healthier. The audience paid a fee to attend and this served as a great fundraiser.

I am always trying to make people feel good about themselves. A great way to do this is a Fashion Show. When people change their eating and exercise habits for the better, they feel great. A fashion show is a great way to show off the results. The admission fee can be used to help support other programs and activities. We had other fashion shows also, but without the dinner.

Support Groups

It gives me great joy to be able to assist those in need. I organized a weekly support group called *Eat Smart - Move More*. The goal was to teach Diabetics how to measure their food and to encourage them to also exercise. We held discussions on their sugar number and their overall health. This group was hosted at the center. It is difficult being a diabetic. You need to know how to take care of yourself. Watching what you eat and how much you eat is a big part of taking proper care of yourself.

Organic Gardens

The Diabetes CORE Group actively worked with REACH US: SEA-CEED, The Bunnelle Foundation, South Carolina Department of Health and Environmental Control, the South Carolina Diabetes Initiative, and local civic organizations to encourage individuals to produce organic gardens.

Objective:

> Encourage and teach community members within the rural area of Georgetown County to practice healthy eating habits through gardening and healthy cooking.

Methods:

- Cultivate a community garden divided into plots to produce organic fruits and vegetables.
- Demonstrate proper gardening techniques.
- Provide cooking classes to demonstrate how to prepare vegetables.
- Provide classes on nutrition and diet to understand proper serving sizes and portions.

Results:

> When taught the proper gardening techniques and skills of cooking healthier, we are expecting the community to be conscious of the food they prepare.
>
> Since the beginning of the garden, the Diabetes CORE Group has planted vegetables

including tomatoes, bell peppers, okras, lima beans, crowder peas, collard greens, and sweet potatoes. The Diabetes CORE Group has distributed over 100 baskets to senior citizens at community centers, and churches, and to the people of the Choppee community. In addition, the vegetables are being used in the Diabetes CORE Group's cooking classes to prepare healthy meals. From the planning stage of the community until now we had approximately 110 volunteers to assist with the garden.

Conclusions:

The lifestyle changes associated with the project include increased physical activity for participants and increase in healthy vegetable consumption for consumers.

My gratitude goes out to our men in the community, both young and old, who brought their tractors and worked the land for us, plowing and tending to the soil, raking the land and helping us to plant the vegetables.

Being Flexible

I remember very well when our committee set up a day of activities to support a particular community. We believed that this community was on board with us. However, when we arrived, to our surprise, they were having their own event – a dinner sale.

We were planning to have a castle with food and games, etc. There was going to be food catering to the tastes of adults and kids. We were also planning to have a health screening.

Rather than going home and being angry, we decided to join in with them and be supportive. After all, we were on a mission to help people live longer. It was not important who held the event.

It is important that we do not allow circumstances to derail us. This work requires flexibility. Friends told me that it was a good thing it was me and not them because they would have been very angry. Well, I was still able to accomplish what I set out to do which was to give information to the community. I saw that as another opportunity for me to help people.

Fundraising

The Diabetes CORE Group does fundraising in the community to assist people with medication for diabetes and other disease related problems, eyeglasses, transportation, etc. – whatever their needs are. When we raise funds, we use it as far as it goes.

When you come in constant contact with low income people, it gives you a different outlook on life. When the community helps, it's a lot easier for those individuals. When I put my small amount of money and others put their small amount of money, and you put it all together, it is amazing what a team can do.

Our fundraising activities have included: Food sales, revival meetings, dinner theaters (The Diabetes CORE Group produced the plays.), banquets, fashion shows, souvenir booklets and just plain *asking*.

Banquets are a great way to raise awareness and raise funds. Once we created a name for ourselves and decided to go full force, we had a kick-off banquet at the beginning of the Diabetes CORE Group's activities, in February of 1998.

This banquet was intended to bring the health care providers and the people in the communities together. It was completely funded by community donations and the residents were able to attend for free.

I simply went around *asking* for donations. People know me and they know that I am honest. So, they were happy to help. The health care providers distributed information to the community by speaking at the event and setting up display tables.

The banquet was a complete success. We were off and running. While this banquet was not a fundraiser, we used it as a guide for future banquets that were fundraisers.

Awareness

Health Fairs

From the beginning, I did presentations at churches and community centers. I also organized and held health fairs with churches and other organizations as well as at the diabetes walks. Tables were set up and information was distributed to the residents of the communities.

Diabetes Walks

We hold diabetes walks to promote awareness of diabetes and related health issues. At the walks, there are vendors, doctors, nurses, health screenings - body fat, blood pressure, etc.

I recalled a diabetes walk where everybody was happy. There were more people there than we had participating in a long time. During the walk, the news came to me, while I was walking, that someone fainted.

They were taken to the hospital, and later died. Ironically, that person had, for the first time, made many phone calls to encourage people to come out to the walk. So, that was a sad time for everyone. I began to pray because I knew what else was coming. In a small community, news travels fast, and not always the way it happened or should be stated. People who were real for God said not to let that stop my work or put a damper on my projects. One brother came to me a few days later and said, "Mrs. Flo, I had to use all kinds of words to a few people who don't even live in the community." He added, "Because you don't want to use profanity. All the good you are trying to do in the community and people are still talking." I said that it didn't bother me because if you look at people that are always criticizing, they are not doing anything to help the community. So, pray for those brothers and sisters, keep the vision, and keep marching. The cost and struggle are too great to be thrown off your journey.

The Diabetes CORE Group went into many areas with workshops and walks. It was not easy getting people to participate in the walks, either. We had to hit the road running. We had to publicize by putting out flyers and talking to many people - radio interviews, TV interviews, church announcements, word of mouth.

When you give information to the community, you must be truthful, honest, and love people. When you give information to the community, people can detect whether you are real or you are just out to get the money. You can't give up and you must not give up. Keep the Faith.

Individual Referrals for Resources

The Diabetes CORE Group encourages people to LEARN ABOUT DIABETES. A great source of information is the local library. In the Georgetown library, residents can find a lot of information on diabetes.

We encourage Georgetown residents to visit the public library and take advantage of the numerous resources. They can get a Georgetown County library card to borrow materials and use services for free.
There is a wealth of information at the library including:

- Books (print and audio)
- Magazines
- Videos
- CDs and DVDs
- Meetings
- Guest Speakers
- Internet
- Databases
- Ask a librarian to help you find information about diabetes.

In addition to visiting the library, people are also encouraged to:

- Learn to prevent diabetes complications
- Work for better diabetes care in our community
- Speak with diabetes educators, dieticians, and nurses about your diabetes
- Share diabetes information
- Learn about diabetes education, nutrition, and exercise programs
- Talk with others about living better with diabetes
- Work to make positive change in diabetes care
- Learn about financial assistance programs for health care

Ask the Doctor

Do you know your number? What is you A1C? What is your cholesterol and what is your blood pressure? We started an educational program called *Ask the Doctor*. It was an ongoing program which was held at the churches. We had a lot of people in attendance. It started out at the church that I attend. Many churches participated. When people go to the doctor, they don't always know what questions to ask. They don't know what information they need. Doctors don't always take the time to explain, voluntarily. I am encouraging people to ask for the information they need from their doctors. I've worked continuously with senior citizens in presentations such as *Ask the Doctor,* so that they can be aware and live better.

Here are questions we encourage people to ask their health provider:

- Do I have diabetes?
- What is my blood pressure?
- What are my blood sugar numbers? What do they mean?
- How often should I check my feet?
- Where can I attend diabetes classes?
- What kind of exercises should I do?
- What can I eat? How often? How much?

Take a Loved One to the doctor Day

This is a day set aside for people who needed assistance to get to the doctor. People were encouraged to take someone to the doctor that they knew needed to see the doctor.

Youth Programs

We used the community garden to teach the youth how to plant, tend and harvest vegetables. In addition, we gave presentations and talks to the youth within the school system while giving out brochures.

Community Support

It is so good when you live in a way that people want to help you. Without the people in the community and the help of God, I would never be able to do the things I do. My heart is so humble when I think of the people who have made my work so easy.

I wish I could do so much more. It breaks my heart when I think about the choice people have to make sometimes, such as: Should I get my medication, or should I go see a doctor, or should I pay my bills?

I met a brother one day who was standing outside a store and he had an amputation. I had a conversation with him. It turns out that he was really trying to decide whether he should get his medication or buy some food. Conversations like this give me the motivation to keep me passing out information on Diabetes and related diseases.

Expanding Our Reach

We continue to expand into new areas educating people about diabetes, high blood pressure and cholesterol, etc. I am reminded of a Saturday morning when I was going into a new area just to look around. We went into this grocery store and I spotted this lady. I went over and began talking to the lady about her health. My question to her was, "Are you a diabetic?" She said yes. I began to tell her about a complete life style change. My daughter said, "Mama, you don't have any shame." Well, diabetes does not exclude anyone and it doesn't see color. It is a serious disease and you have to take care of it and follow doctors' orders. Diabetes has no shame.

11

AWARDS & RECOGNITION

When I got our community involved in diabetes education, we didn't know what to expect or what to ask for. But the Diabetes CORE Group was born and has done great work. People are living healthier lives and there has been a reduction in amputations. Dr. Carolyn Jenkins of MUSC REACH 2010 said that in Georgetown County, the number of African-American male amputees has been reduced by approximately 50%. I, myself, have survived cancer and I live a full life while living with diabetes, high blood pressure, and glaucoma. My life has been a very active life. I have several illnesses, but I am a believer in the God I serve. I believe that if I do all that I can, He will do the rest.

June, 2017 will be 20 years since I began taking on "my destiny with diabetes." We will have a banquet celebrating the occasion in September, 2017. Thousands of people have been helped, and the Diabetes CORE Group has been recognized nationwide by many organizations.

To my amazement, I have personally received numerous awards, certificates, and plaques along the way because of my work with the Diabetes CORE Group.

I am very proud of our efforts and I wish to encourage others to start something in their communities. You don't need a PhD. You just need to care about people and be willing to work. People will join in and help.

The task of helping people who are dealing with diabetes is a job that always needs more willing workers. It is my hope that this book will inspire anyone with a desire to help to do just that - help. It might seem really small at first, but just start something and watch it grow – like an acorn. I am convinced that you can make a big difference no matter who you are. I did, even though I quit school at age 12.

I feel so blessed because God has allowed me to do so many things in the field of health with a limited education. My passion and love for people has really carried me places I never expected to go.

Below, you will find some of our awards and recognition. These honors testify to the impact that a small idea can make.

A Retirement Surprise

Four years after I originally planned on retiring, I finally retired. January 3, 2008, was retirement day for me. I reached 65 years of age and I retired from MUSC REACH 2010.

I had a great retirement party. About 250-300 people were in attendance. That was such a surprise for me, but not as surprising as what was to follow 4 days later.

On January 7, 2008, I was presented with the prestigious *Order of the Palmetto* award from the State of South Carolina. Not many civilians are given the *Order of the Palmetto* award. This is the highest honor that can be presented to a civilian in the State of South Carolina. What a great honor to be received upon retirement.

I was thrilled that the Governor's office thought that my contributions were of "statewide significance." But I am aware that I did not do it alone. I had the cooperation of a host of people and the favor of God. I know that God was with me. Wow! To God be the glory.

My work gives me a lot of visibility. People from all over are watching my activities. As a result, being a member of the South Carolina Silver Haired Legislature (SCSHL) is another great honor that has been bestowed upon me. The SCSHL was created by statute for the following purpose: *To identify issues, concerns and possible solutions for problems faced, with emphasis on issues related to seniors; to make recommendations to the governor and to members of the South Carolina General Assembly; And to educate the public on senior issues.* This is good because I constantly come in contact with seniors as well as being a senior myself.

I helped to organize many communities with information on diabetes and I received many awards for that. The *Hettie Richardson Award* was one such award.

One day, I received a call from a company saying that there was an award being given in North Carolina and they felt that I could win that award, based on the work I was doing in Georgetown. We applied for the award and I won for community work.

During the course of my regular activities, I was approached and asked, by one of the administrators at the Georgetown Library, if I wanted to go to Atlanta to represent Georgetown in a competition. I said, "Sure!"

I was one of several presenters that went on this trip from Georgetown County. My presentation was on the creation of the Choppee Health Complex. Well, we came back with an award. My presentation, for the Choppee Health Complex, won. My county, Georgetown County, was honored with the designation "All American City" by the National Civic League. This award can be won by neighborhoods, towns, villages, cities, counties, or regions. There were 48 states represented. We finished in tenth place. Someone said to me afterwards, "We won because you made the presentation." I just laughed. I don't know. Maybe.

Requests to appear on television shows, to speak at various events and to give interviews for various magazines and newspapers have also come my way, as well as being featured in a book.

It was an honor to be featured in the book, *Cheating Destiny* by James S. Hirsch - a book about diabetes. In this book, I was referred to as "The Diabetes Queen." It was an extreme honor to know that my work had spread so far that it would bring someone to my country neighborhood to write about my work and put it in a book. Just like me, he has advised people to know their numbers. Just because you are a diabetic does not mean your life is over.

You alone are in control of your health. And your health is the most important thing.

I remember being asked to go on ETV in Columbia, S.C. and talk about the work we do in the community and the education we received through the MUSC REACH 2010 program. I said to myself, "A person of my small status going on a television panel with all those PhD's and every kind of letters before and behind their names?" I could only say, "Thank you, Lord." I was with a panel of Bishops, politicians and community leaders. There were times when I just had to say, "Lord, please give me the strength to go through with this program." But when you are doing something for others, it feels better than doing it just for yourself. God Bless.

Another TV show invited me to come on the air to discuss work that was being done in a county-wide research project to improve stroke outcome in Georgetown County. The Diabetes CORE Group and MUSC REACH 2010, we never backed away from any challenge. My daughter-in-law, Joyce Linnen, along with Dr. Carolyn Jenkins and CEASEL worked with me on this research project.

Everyone who knows me knows that I always believe in telling the truth and being honest. Once, when I went to do a presentation, in Charleston, S.C., this young, well educated, person said to me, "These are dignitaries, so you can't say anything about religion to them." I said, "Thank you very much for that information." Now, I could hardly pronounce these people names, let alone spell their names. But when I got up to speak, I started the conversation by saying to the panel, "To God be the Glory!" I believe in getting it into your heart.

Another time, I was preparing to be on a panel with government officials in Charleston, S.C. I think this was called a Caucus Board, or something like that. (It's been almost 20 years. It's hard to remember all the details.) I said to myself again, "Lord, all these people." But I kept my mind on who got me there and who I was representing. I was representing God and the people. I held my ground and it all went smoothly. Keeping your focus goes a long way.

A Winning Team

I am very proud of the Diabetes CORE Group. Our work has been done entirely with volunteers and donations. People have given selflessly and these awards and recognition are a tribute to all of them. I can only imagine what we could accomplish, if we had a full time, paid staff. Never the less, we do what we can with what we have and we do it from the heart. I know that just by participating in, and going to workshops and conferences has helped me a lot, as well as many other people.

The Georgetown County Diabetes CORE Group was recognized nationally for their excellence in working to improve health and computer literacy. This was a project done in partnership with MUSC REACH 2010. The award was presented by the National Networks of Libraries of Medicine. I must say that when this project was introduced to me, one of the workers said, "Use your mouse." I said, "The only mouse I know is a mouse in the barn." I was being sarcastic, but those ladies stayed with me until I learned how to navigate the computer. We were taught by the librarian of Carver's Bay High School and some assistants.

We were taught how to look up health information, and how to research their (National Networks of Libraries of Medicine) medicine and its effects. Initially, there were about 7 or 8 of us in training. Once we learned, we proceeded to train the community.

There were seven persons from MUSC REACH 2010 and the Diabetes CORE Group who attended this award presentation. We traveled to Bethesda, Maryland for the event. There were 48 states represented and we came in 1st place. You should have seen all of us praying together so that we would win. We were some happy people.

We, the Georgetown County Diabetes CORE Group, work collaboratively with the Diabetes Initiative of South Carolina and have received many leading awards. One award was the American Diabetes Association Community Leaders Promising Practice Award (2009).

The Diabetes CORE Group has won the award for the best poster presentation at the Diabetes Symposium and National Meeting in Charleston, S.C. We created a chart depicting the work that we do. And we won for excellence in working with communities to improve diabetes outcome. To God be the Glory for all the great things he has done. The Diabetes CORE Group went every year and won several times.

MUSC REACH 2010 has really trained us well. The Diabetes CORE Group and MUSC REACH 2010 received the National Community-Campus Partnership for Health Award (2006): Pastor for Health Services Research, National Diabetes Translation Conference.

In connection with this event, the Diabetes CORE Group members were trained at workshops in many cities—Chicago; Seattle; Washington, D.C.; Boston; Bethesda, MD; as well as training throughout South Carolina. We learned a lot from the workshops at these conferences.

I am grateful for Dr. Carolyn Jenkins, who gave me the opportunity to work in the area of Diabetes health care on an expanded basis. And even though her program - REACH 2010 - ended, she still supports the Diabetes CORE Group.

Additionally, I am grateful to MUSC REACH 2010, Dr. Jenkins and the County of Georgetown, South Carolina for giving me a chance to educate the communities of Georgetown County. In doing so, I got to travel to many places and was privileged to work on the board of directors of many organizations. When I look at my background, it still amazes me.

The MUSC REACH 2010 has empowered me to fulfill my passion of helping the community with their health needs. I am truly grateful to them.

These were just some of the awards and recognition that the Georgetown County Diabetes CORE Group and I have received. We have plaques all over my office at the Choppee Health Complex as well as posters in the office and out in the hallway. They really belong to the communities. They contributed to our success from their heart.

12

10 - YEAR MILESTONE

At our 10-year anniversary, I recalled that less than 2 days after the *Diabetes Today* workshop that changed my life, I came back and talked to my church about it and began a small group from there. After 10 years, there were seven groups in the communities hearing the latest in diabetes news from doctors and nutritionists, forming walking groups, and looking out for one another.

It has been such a blessing for me to see that I can have diabetes and live a normal healthy life.

In addition to the people participating in programs to improve their health, by 2007, the Diabetes CORE

Group had received its 5013c. That is great because our donors can now deduct their donations.

Furthermore, it is very exciting to be housed in the building that used to be our high school – The Choppee Health Complex. We were educated there as kids. Now, we are educated there for our health.

I remember my father saying to me, "If you continue to work the way you do, not only will you have one office, you'll have two offices." Guess what, I ended up having two offices. My father was right again.

In 2017, we will celebrate the 20-year anniversary of the Georgetown County Diabetes CORE Group. Several people who started with me or joined in along the way, have now passed on. But their contribution will always be appreciated.

I am now in my 70s. It is my hope to find a successor to continue as director of the Diabetes CORE Group. While I did start it, I won't be around forever. Being that this is not a paid position, finding a successor is a difficult task. We do not have funding to pay a staff. Hopefully, in the future, that will change. In the meantime, I am encouraging others to pick up the mantle and run with it in their own communities. There is great need and every little bit helps.

As of this writing, I am a thirteen year survivor of cancer and I live with high blood pressure and diabetes, and I am still going strong. I feel so blessed because God has allowed me to do so many things in the field of health with limited education. To God be the Glory for all the great things he has done. I think the next thing I will do is get my GED. That would be great.

As the director of the Georgetown County Diabetes CORE Group, I have been invited to more places to speak than I could attend, and I am continually invited to be on various boards of directors. I have traveled all over the United States, and I have sat and talked about health care with government officials in Columbia, S.C. and in our nation's capital, Washington, D.C. When I think of my background, how I have gone from picking cotton for 3 cents a lb. to discussing healthcare in the capitol, with no formal education beyond the 6th grade, I am convinced that anyone can do what I did and make a difference in their community. That includes you.

As I have said before, my heart is to see people happy. Know that I love each and every one of you. Take care of your health and help your community.

Quotes about the Diabetes CORE Group

"The Diabetes CORE Group is a model for programs across the state."
— Former SC First Lady, Mary Wood Beasley

"Diabetes CORE Group is one of the perfect examples of a community effort that helps others. This is a spark for other communities."
—Ted Brown, former Representative, Georgetown, S.C.

"I've been following the Diabetes CORE Group and I've learned a lot about how to take care of myself. The CORE Group has also established walking groups around the county, and I always go along with the one in my neighborhood. We talk as we walk and I've learned more about what to eat and not eat, and how to prevent diabetes."
— Julia Brockington of Brown's Ferry

"Our old school has a new purpose and is again the heart of the community."
— Florene Linnen

PART III

SUMMARY

At A Glance

A lot of work and time has gone into the development of the Diabetes CORE Group. I am giving you, in this book, somewhat of an overview. This section seeks to give you a condensed view which is intended to be a readily available reference for anyone seeking to use this group as a template to begin something in their own community.

Here, I reiterate the work, but in the form of bullets and lists for a bird's eyes view of what we have done. Feel free to use any of these ideas for activities or events.

I believe that the recognition we received speaks to the success of our endeavors. And I hope that they will serve as reassurances that the activities that I am suggesting to you are indeed sound ideas and not just talk. It is not my desire to "toot my own horn." But I don't know of any other way to inspire you to join those who have followed our example at the Diabetes CORE Group and to start something in your community.

This is important: do not be intimidated by lack of a diploma or a degree, or money, etc. Start from where you are. People need what you have to offer.

Defining the Diabetes CORE Group

The Georgetown County Diabetes CORE Group is a community initiative created to address the need for more education and awareness programs for persons with diabetes and related illnesses. The Diabetes CORE Group collaborates with other community organizations, institutions, and government agencies to help people with diabetes, their family, and friends.

Diabetes CORE Group Purpose
• Diabetes Education • Empowerment • Advocacy • Change the Health System

A Quote from the 1ST Anniversary Celebration

"Believe in yourself.

In the power you have to control your life day to day.

Believe in the strength that you have deep inside,

And your faith will help show you the way,

Believe in tomorrow and what it will bring,

Let a hopeful heart carry you through,

For things will work out if you trust and believe,

There's no limit to what you can do!"

- from the Diabetes CORE Group's First Anniversary Program, September 15, 1998

Community Activities & Classes

- Diabetes Education
- Computer Health Classes
- Healthy Cooking Classes
- Fitness and Wellness Class
- Nutrition Education Programs
- Support Groups
- Organic Gardens
- Fundraising
- Health Fairs
- Diabetes Walk
- Individual Referrals for Resources
- Ask the doctor
- Take a Loved One to the Doctor Day
- Youth Programs

Diabetes CORE Group Events List

Here I have listed events from the first 10 years. Many of these events have become recurring events either annually or intermittently. They are all joint efforts to some degree. Joining forces with other organizations can give your efforts a great boost.

Diabetes CORE Group-The First 10 Years

- June 27-28, 1997. In Myrtle Beach, S.C. Ms. Florene Linnen successfully completed training for *Diabetes Today*, a course for community leaders. Ms. Linnen began to talk to the congregation at Nazareth AME, where she found a great number of people with diabetes, which was a big concern for her. She began to reach out to other churches and organizations.

- September 15, 1997. First General Meeting of the Diabetes CORE Group at Dickerson AME Church in Georgetown. 76 people attended. The Group was named "Diabetes Community Outreach Resource Education (CORE) Group."

- October 13, 1997. Second meeting at Mt. Lebanon AME Church, County Line Road, Andrews, S.C. 27 people attended.

- November 8, 1997. *Diabetes Walk for Health*. Sponsored by the Diabetes CORE Group, SC DHEC Waccamaw Health District, Georgetown Memorial Hospital, and South Carolina's First lady's Women's Health Campaign. Mrs. Mary Wood Beasley, wife of then Governor Beasley, was a guest. The Health Walk became an annual event.

- November 20, 1997. Third General Meeting, Nazareth AME Church. 31 people attended.

    Ms. Linnen began coordinating monthly workshops at churches, community centers, and any place where the Diabetes CORE Group was invited throughout

Georgetown.

- March 26, 1998. First Diabetes CORE Group Banquet in Georgetown, S.C. The banquet was made possible through donations from the community. The banquet became an annual event.

- May 2, 1998. Diabetes University, East Bay Park, S.C. Sponsored by Eli Lilly, Inc. and Diabetes CORE Group with support in part by the Medical University of South Carolina, SC DHEC Waccamaw District, and Georgetown Memorial Hospital.

- July 18, 1998. Diabetes CORE Group's First Annual Health Fair and Walk-a-thon. The First Lady's Health Campaign. 100 people attended.

  "It is important to walk against diabetes. It's important to be committed and stand tall to educate the residents of our community and to take control of this problem – from head to toe." – Ms. Florene Linnen

- September 15, 1998. First Anniversary Celebration of the Georgetown County Diabetes CORE Group at Nazareth AME Church.

- December 1998. Easter Seals of Georgetown County sponsors diabetic supplies for one diabetic per month per Ms. Linnen's request representing the Diabetes CORE Group.

- November 6, 1999. The first REACH 2010 Partners Meeting was the start of a strong working relationship with Dr. Carolyn Jenkins and the REACH 2010 Charleston and

Georgetown Diabetes Coalition.

- June 3, 2005. The Diabetes CORE Group received 501(3) (c) tax-exempt status.

- March 21, 2005. Choppee Health Complex had its Grand Opening Ceremony.

- March 10, 2007. 10th Anniversary Diabetes Banquet Celebration at Brown's Ferry Elementary School auditorium.

Awards & Recognitions Lists

When I think of all the awards and various recognition that the Diabetes CORE Group and I have received, I am absolutely amazed. But knowing how it happened excites me because I realize that it does not take a genius. Anyone can do it. We are just ordinary people. I know I keep saying it, but I am proud of my volunteers and donors.

Below are some of the recognition we have received over the years. I hope that you will start something and receive some recognition yourself. It would make my heart glad to know that you did.

The Diabetes CORE Group

- April 27, 2006. *"Pat-On-The-Back" Volunteer Award* presented to Georgetown County Diabetes COORE Group by The South Carolina Public Health Association and Public Health Region 6

- May 3, 2006. The REACH Library Partnership won the US National Commission on Libraries and Information Science, *2006 Libraries & Health Information Award grand prize*, Presented at the National Library of Medicine, Bethesda, MD.

- June 5, 2006. REACH Charleston and Georgetown Diabetes Coalition won the *2006 Community-Campus Partnerships for Health Award* presented at the Community-Campus Partnerships for Health Annual Meeting in Minneapolis, MN.

- June 25, 2006 Georgetown County was named one of 10 *All-American City* communities in the nation by the National Civic League in Atlanta, GA.

- We the Georgetown County Diabetes CORE Group work collaboratively with the Diabetes Initiative of South Carolina and have received the *American Diabetes Association community leaders promising Practice Award* (2009)

- Received an *award from National Coalition for Excellence* for working with communities to improve diabetes outcome.

- Diabetes CORE has won the *Best Poster award* at the Diabetes Symposium and National Meeting several times.

Florene Linnen

- Appeared on ETV and other stations and talked about the work done in the community and the education received through the Reach 2010 program.

- Featured in the book *Cheating Destiny – Living with diabetes* by James S. Hirsch as "The Diabetes Queen."

- November 22, 1999. Commended and honored by the South Carolina House of Representatives for her work with the Georgetown County Diabetes CORE Group, citing that her work has set this group apart from all others, making it a first – class organization, working for the betterment of all citizens in Georgetown County.

- 2000. Recognized by the South Carolina State Senate for performing outstanding community work.

- *Hettie Rickett Award* for Outstanding Volunteer Community Service from the South Carolina Community Development Association 2001-2002.

- 2003. Recipient of the Alston/Banneman Fellowship Award.

- Received a plaque "in recognition of your untiring efforts and dedication as Chairperson of the Board of Directors for St. James – Santee Family Health Center 1999-2004. "

- August 9, 2007. *Certificate of Recognition* from the African

Methodist Episcopal Church to Sis. Florene Linnen in recognition of dedicated service to the ministry of God as the *Health Director* for the Georgetown District .

- Recognition by the County of Williamsburg, South Carolina for outreach work in the communities. Received at retirement.

- 2007. Recognition by the NAACP for outstanding work with the Georgetown County Diabetes CORE Group.

- January 2008. Recognized by the Senate of the state of South Carolina.

- January 7, 2008. Presented with the *Order of the Palmetto -* South Carolina's highest Award presented to civilians.

- 2010. Featured in the *Diabetes Forecast – The Healthy Living Magazine.*

- 2016. Featured in *Diabetic Living Magazine* as "A Warrior for Health."

- A member of the *South Carolina Silver Haired Legislature* (SCSHL). The SCSHL was created by statute for the following purpose: To identify issues, concerns and possible solutions for problems faced by emphasis on issues related to seniors. To make recommendations to the governor and to members of the South Carolina General Assembly and to educate the public on senior issues.

Start something in your community. There is no telling how many people you will help, or how many people will help you.

For More Information, or to donate to the Georgetown County Diabetes CORE Group,

Contact:

Florene Linnen

Georgetown County Diabetes CORE Group

Choppee Health Complex

8189 Choppee Road

Georgetown, SC 29440

Website:

www.georgetowncountydiabetes.com

Facebook:

www.facebook.com/ gcdiabetescore

FLORENE LINNEN

www.ingramcontent.com/pod-product-compliance
Lightning Source LLC
Chambersburg PA
CBHW031417290426
44110CB00011B/425